from Ad and Mary
November 1997

THE ACTRESS AND
THE BREWER'S WIFE

Also by Virginia Surtees

THE ACTRESS AND
THE BREWER'S WIFE

Two Victorian Vignettes

VIRGINIA SURTEES

MICHAEL RUSSELL

E

Time remembered is grief forgotten

First published in Great Britain 1997
by Michael Russell (Publishing) Ltd
Wilby Hall, Wilby, Norwich NR 16 2JP

Typeset in Sabon by The Typesetting Bureau
Allen House, East Borough, Wimborne, Dorset
Printed and bound in Great Britain
by Biddles Ltd, Guildford and King's Lynn

Contents

CONTENTS

List of Illustrations

Acknowledgements

To Her Majesty the Queen for gracious permission to publish two letters from Albert Edward Prince of Wales.

For the first part of this book my special thanks go to my two cousins, Miss Pamela Tower and Mr Jack Bayley, for recollections they had heard in connection with our great-grandmother and to which my late sister, Evangeline Bruce, added considerably. To these I would add Miss Rosalind Pulver, without whose information and continued interest in John Downs Rochfort this story could scarcely have been written. To Miss Emma Hicks whose research has helped to trace some of Miss Herbert's wayward steps I am immeasurably grateful, as I am to Mr Jack Reading to whose theatre knowledge I owe much; to the late Mr Anthony Butler and Mrs Butler; Mr Maldwin Drummond; Mrs Betty Elzea; the late Mrs Frank Gee; Mrs Charlotte Gere; Dr David Hay; Mr Myles Thoroton Hildyard, himself a kinsman of John Rochfort; Mr J. G. Links; Sir Anthony Milbank, Bt, a great-grandson of a hero of this tale; the late Mr George Nash, Enthoven Collection, Victoria and Albert Museum, under whose guiding hand I worked for three years; Mrs Harold Rossetti. I warmly thank Mr Lionel Lambourne; Mrs J. Lumsden; Mrs Katharine Macdonald; Mr Michael Meredith; Dr

Graham Storey; Major-General Sir John Swinton; Sir Geoffrey Trevelyan, Bt; and Dame Gillian Wagner for their assistance from which I have benefited.

In recording the life of Valerie Meux I wish to thank Mr Peter Rooke for his unfailing help, which has been invaluable in both providing me with a great deal of information in his editorship of *Theobalds through the Centuries* as well as pointing the way to further essential material; in much of this I am also greatly obliged to Mr Ronald Mott. The Earl of Cardigan has given me permission to quote from the Ailesbury archives for which I am grateful, as I am to Mr Michael Marsham and the staff of the Wiltshire Record Office for making these papers available to me. Mr Bernard Mould, of Enfield Property Services, was generous with his time and knowledge concerning Theobalds; Mr Hugh Massingberd has also been of assistance, as has Dr Nigel Thorp, Glasgow University Library, to whom I am indebted. I thank Miss Hester Barron; Mr J. D. Callaghan, Hancocks & Co. Ltd, regarding Lady Meux's diamond buckle; Miss Eileen Blemkin and Mrs Jacky Green of Hertford Local Studies who have helped me over various points and Rodney Todd-White & Son who have used their skill with several of the illustrations. So many have given so generously of their time that I can only record my sincere apologies should their kindness not be properly acknowledged here.

Introduction

Owing to the times in which they lived, the sketches of these two ambitious women of different generations, though both Victorians, are incomplete. They held two characteristics in common – both were equally obsessively secretive about their backgrounds and their ages. Because the actress gained admirers and friends in the aristocracy, at which she aimed, as well as in the upper echelons of Society, it was imperative that she should hint at a certain refinement of background. For the brewer's wife it was essential to hide all conjecture of an irregular parentage and upbringing in the hope of being accepted in the magic circle of Society. In this she failed, although Whistler's portraits of her have in a sense atoned for that exclusion by perpetuating her memory long after most of her social superiors have been forgotten; much as Dante Gabriel Rossetti's images of the actress (seventeen of which were in her possession at the time of her death) have accorded her too a kind of arcane immortality.

Mr Richard Dorment interested me in Lady Meux and suggested I might find her an entertaining individual for biography. Mr Peter Rooke as editor and Mr R. Mott with their account of *Theobalds through the Centuries* made the suggestion irresistible.

Of Miss Herbert the actress, my great-grandmother, I have

wished to write something for many years. In PreRaphaelite legend there has been a curiosity to know more and in the history of the English stage there is little knowledge beyond the roles she undertook. She so far outlived her contemporaries that there was no one to question either among her acquaintance or in her immediate family, where to have been an actress – even to the first quarter of this century – was scarcely to be mentioned. Her late conversion to Rome indicated repentance and with it came destruction of all letters and papers and, so far as she was able, suppression of information regarding her life. Again, she was pretty thorough.

I have sifted what nuggets of information I have been able to collect over a long period and allied them to the joint recollections of my late sister and two cousins, rejecting – perhaps mistakenly – what seemed exaggerations, such as the claim that as a very young girl Miss Herbert 'went round the world in a sailing boat', or that she was a member of Hengler's Equestrian Company; although owing to her duplicity anything is possible.

The Actress

I

Miss Herbert's Début

J ohn Maynard had his roots in Tiverton, Devon, but the formative years of his four daughters, Sarah, Jane, Louisa Ruth and Emma, were spent in Bristol where, so far as can be accurately established before the advent of birth registration but at least according to public census returns, they were born during the 1820s and into the next decade. Their mother Fanny (Frances) was from Somerset. There had been a son, John, an apprentice on a merchant vessel who disappeared at sea from the yardarm, it was said. All that remained of the young life was his brass-bound sea chest and his unhappy mother's certainty that he had been pushed overboard by a jealous captain.

John Maynard's trade was never specified but his death certificate pronounced him a brass founder and coppersmith, both decently acceptable but in an age of rare snobbishness 'gentleman' was a seemly addition. Dying in 1871 at the age of eighty-five, he had given his daughters an adequate education, cheap enough at the time, with funds said to have been derived from transactions in the Napoleonic Wars. Subsequently, in the thriving industries of Bristol and the West Country there were openings for trading in the production of brass and Maynard may have held a situation in Harford's Bristol Brass and Copper Company in Corn Street, or the Freeman & Copper Company of Small Street, another large and important concern. But whether indeed we are mistaken in supposing he had any such position or whether it was owing to the decline of Bristol's prosperity in the 1840s, the family had to face a degree of poverty and the daughters were obliged to seek employment. They wrote a good copperplate hand, had some knowledge of French and could sew and embroider, sufficient preparation for governessing or dressmaking, kindred occupations of subjugation for females seeking work.

However, no preparation whatsoever had been made on the parents' part to contend with the ambition and determination of their third daughter. To their horror Louisa Ruth 'ran away from home to go on the stage'; chucking respectability to the dogs, preferring the stigma of scandal to an inconspicuous life of moral scruples. For to be an actress was synonymous with prostitution and no doubt Louisa had been lured to her first trivial 'engagement' through the influence of a lover. It was about the only way that would-be actresses got work, at a time when more and more women aspired to a theatrical career.

As 'Miss Herbert', the name by which she is best known, she appeared at the Lyceum Theatre on 1 December 1847 making her '1st appearance' as Cecily Evans, 5th Milliner in *Peggy Green*, a 'new Comic Drama', and thereafter on 1 January 1848 in *Bowers of Arcadia*, with a 'Fête al Fresco', an 'Arcadian Mazurka-Polka and a Pastoral Gallopade'. Here she was one of sixteen dancers dressed in costumes designed by 'the most Rococo Authorities in China'. For most of February she played Emeline Emden in *Astounding Phenomena!*, 'an original, mesmeric sketch, an amusing and laughable trifle'.

The Lyceum had newly reopened, its interior embellished and reconstructed, the dress circle replacing the balcony, according to *The Era*. The 'dazzling' Madame Vestris was the manageress, her husband, Charles James Mathews, son of the famous comedian, the lessee. Early in her career she had married first Armand Vestris, Italian like herself, *premier danseur* at the King's Theatre. As a singer she had appeared many times at Covent Garden but by 1827 with advancing years (she was then about thirty) her operatic career was coming to an end and she had adopted the stage. Her ambition was to make the Lyceum the most fashionable theatre in London and in this she succeeded. The house was thronged nightly and was accorded a special cachet by the visit of Queen Victoria. *The Era* noted that Lord and Lady Ernest Bruce 'have lately honoured the theatre with their patronage' and here lay the origin of a long intimacy. Lord Ernest Brudenell-Bruce, who in 1878 succeeded his father as 3rd Marquess of Ailesbury, was one of the few who called Louisa by that name to the end of his life and would still be visiting her familiarly forty years later.

The girl who came romping onto the stage as 5th Milliner on that December night, 1847, was born in 1831 according to her marriage certificate, but since with the multiplication of years her age contracted this may not have been wholly accurate. Tall and graceful with corn-yellow hair and large azure eyes, a long neck and already the strongly defined jaw epitomising the determination and stubbornness which were to carry her towards her goal, at sixteen she showed no particular ability as a burgeoning actress. Indeed, throughout her career she reflected Ellen Terry's dictum of some years later: 'She was not a remarkable actress, but her appearance was wonderful indeed', affecting the 'spiritual ethereal look which the aesthetic movement loved'.[1]

After her performances at the Lyceum she disappears:

maybe she was touring the provinces in very minor parts, maybe, as rumour had it, she was married to a man for a year who died of galloping consumption, that prevailing Victorian malady. That she had an affair with T. W. Robertson (a *péché de jeunesse*) can likewise not be verified and seems unlikely. She does not reappear for another six years and whatever occurrences had constituted her life in the interval, from now to the grave her deliberate secrecy and invention blur the facts. Respectability demanded no less. She falsified events and dates and hid all indication of her background, giving out, down to the second generation, that her father had been a clergyman (quite a usual allegation amongst women of scandalous repute) – there was even the hint (no more than that but put out by herself) that she was the daughter of a Somerset squire. It had been said that a mist ordinarily surrounded the beginnings of a theatrical career and that an actor was born wherever it pleased him, and with these observations Miss Herbert was in complete accord. What was irrefutably true however, according to the census returns of 1851, and for whatever the cause, John Maynard, now no more than a labourer at a brass foundry (perhaps he had never been more than that), was living with his wife Fanny in a cramped cottage at Flowers Terrace, Limehouse, sharing with a lodger employed as a 'labourer in a gasworks'. At this period there were several brassfounders operating from Limehouse where Maynard probably found work. Jane Maynard, the unmarried second daughter, nine years older than Louisa, lived with her parents, earning some kind of livelihood as a dressmaker. The eldest daughter, Sarah, said to have had galloping consumption, had sailed for Australia probably in the hopes of a cure and employment. On the sailing ship she met a passenger with the same disease, married him and lived in Australia in some affluence, with no further reports of illness. It had also been surmised (perhaps only by Mrs Maynard) that Sarah might find some trace of the son John who had fallen overboard but could somehow have survived to find a haven in the southern hemisphere.

Emma Maynard, the youngest of the sisters and Louisa's favourite, did rather well for herself. Born in Bristol but possibly working in London, she married John Pottow in July 1854 at Holy Trinity, Brompton, with her unmarried sister Jane as a witness. The Pottows came originally from Potterne in Wiltshire and had settled in Bristol. Son of a publican, John Pottow worked a thriving business in the pawnbroking line. Living and working in Lower Maudlin Street, St James's, Bristol, he was part of the firm of Cole and Pottow who also carried on trade as silversmiths and outfitters. Pottow was said to have been the first man to introduce ready-made suits.

Towards the late 1860s Bristol saw a recovery in its economy and Pottow's hard work was crowned with affluence and fifteen children. He moved the family to higher and more salubrious ground on Cotham Brow where Emma was treated to a paddock and her own horses. Edingworth Villa is standing today, renamed and divided into two, but once large enough to accommodate the whole family in its four storeys.

As with everything to do with the Maynards, Emma's age is uncertain. On her marriage certificate in 1854 she gave it as twenty-one, which would suggest her birth in 1833; seventeen years later in the 1871 public census she has become thirty-four, putting her birth at 1837. Her death certificate (1878) places it at 1835.

That Louisa was not a witness at her sister's marriage might indicate that she was away on tour. She re-emerged at

Bristol at the end of 1854, acting in her native town for the first time and for one performance only 'under the not too dignified auspices of an animal-trainer whose family kept a Cider House where women and children were not admitted'.[2] This individual was James Doughty, the famous clown in circus and pantomime and a minor actor. At his Benefit on 15 November at the Theatre Royal he introduced Miss Herbert as Violante, the lead in *The Wonder! Or A Woman Keeps a Secret!*, a comedy in five acts and the plot 'truly Spanish'. In the course of the evening 'Mr Doughty will introduce his PERFORMING DOGS', a Bristol engagement, one can assume, most readily forgotten by the heroine.

At the Glasgow Theatre Royal, Dunlop Street, the popular comedian J. L. Toole made a memorable appearance for one night on 30 April 1855 in a farce, *Boots at the Swan*, in which Miss Herbert played Cecilia Moonshine. Two months earlier she had taken the part of Ophelia opposite Charlotte Saunders, the female Hamlet, a skilled actress who often took male roles.

Two months later Louisa was married.

2

The Olympic, Wych Street

Of Edward Crabb little is known. Where or how he picked up Louisa or whether it was she who made the advances remains obscure.

Born in 1829 at Temple Dinsley, near Hitchen, Hertfordshire, the boy was the youngest of seven children of a well-to-do banker who also had interests in malting and brewing; he died in 1830.

Louisa was married at Holy Trinity, Brompton on 23 June 1855, giving her age as twenty-four, of no profession and a resident of Brompton. Her husband was simply a 'gentleman' of twenty-six years, also resident in Brompton. If not already a stockbroker, he soon would be, working for Barnett, Ellis & Co., 18 Finch Lane. The names given as witnesses are unfamiliar.

From Holy Trinity, Brompton, Louisa's matrimonial path of ostensible virtue led her to her first engagement at the Strand Theatre in October 1855. With her keenness for dissimulation and with an eye to propriety, her name was introduced in the cast list as making her '1st appearance in London' in *Simpson & Co.*, thus relegating to limbo her excursion to the Lyceum Theatre or any recollection of how she had got there. This was a fairly safe gambit, as eight years onward there could have been few people to remember 'Miss Herbert', once cast in the lowly role of the 5th Milliner.

Standing on the south side of the thoroughfare, beyond
Somerset House and on the corner of Surrey Street, the
Strand Theatre was a small structure that had begun as a
Panorama and in 1820 was spoken of as 'near the new
church in the Strand' (St Mary-le-Strand, then only a
hundred years old, was still a newcomer compared to her
much older sister down the road, St Clement Danes). There
was no gallery and the boxes were at four shillings; on the
whole it was not a successful theatre until the end of the
1850s. But for Louisa it had presented an incalculable
benefit: while acting there her superb looks were noticed and
admired. In mid-February 1856 the PreRaphaelite artist.
Dante Gabriel Rossetti first discovered her and was captivated by her beauty. It was most likely on this occasion
when seeing her on the stage that he made a quick outline
of her head, giving the impression of movement, the hair,
the long neck, the too prominent nose always distinctive,
coarsening at the end, usually disguised by the artist but
nevertheless unmistakable and an aid to identification. Rossetti graced the scrap of paper with an enlargement of his
own handwriting across the bottom: 'Stunner No 1'. However, it would be two years before he succeeded in getting her
to sit for him. Following his elation at this first visual
encounter he went again to the theatre on 18 February when
she was playing Laura Leeson in *Time Tries All*, a favourite
comedietta, and a farce *Never Despair*. On 3 March, on
Rossetti's insistent recommendation, Ford Madox Brown
took his wife Emma 'to the Strand Theatre to see Miss
Herbert a discovery of D. G. Rossetti's. She is lovely.'[3] They
would have witnessed a contrived arrangement of *The Merchant of Venice*, Louisa cast as Portia. A critic commented on
'her powers of delivery in the well-known trial scene, upon

which', he reported a shade too plausibly, 'the curtain
dropped.'4

For actresses, whatever their standing, theatre life was a
hard grind. Louisa was no slouch; in three months she had
played seven different parts, chiefly light domestic comedietta, burlesque or farce. The constant changing of the
bill, the memorising of each new part, long rehearsals,
low wages, the confection of theatrical costumes, the late
return home (in Louisa's case from the Strand to Kensington), were trials redeemed by unlimited ambition. In
May 1856 she was fortunate in securing work at the Olympic Theatre in Wych Street, under Alfred Wigan's management.

The Aldwych, as it is called today, was then a warren of
small stinking streets and alleys of disrepute bearing south-
wards from the disease-ridden 'rookeries' of St Giles, known
as the most degrading slums in Britain. These rookeries
comprised small courts housing brothels, criminals, dregs of
humanity and all that was most depraved. Wych Street, more
a lane than a street, dirty, evil-smelling and notorious for
its houses of ill-fame, houses masquerading as cigar shops
opened by females while sheltering thieves' kitchens, was one
of the oldest of these thoroughfares leading from the north
side of the Strand up towards Drury Lane and the slum
district. Newcastle Street was part of this network and
Holywell Street below but running parallel with Wych Street
was purveyor-in-chief of well-displayed pornography. To add
to this squalor the windows in the gabled houses with
overhanging fronts of a much earlier period were usually
obscured by the mud and filth thrown up by the passing cabs.
G. A. Sala, witty, wise and well-informed and hideously ugly,
reported that in all this labyrinth of streets there was none

Holywell Street, now Aldwych

dirtier, narrower, more disreputable in London than that to which Louisa was bound.

The Olympic Theatre, standing on irregularly-shaped ground at the corner of Wych Street and Newcastle Street, once the site of the magnificent Craven House (now Bush House), was the third theatre of that name to occupy the same plot. Burnt down early in 1849 it had opened again, newly built, on Boxing Day of the same year, 'a very oasis in a desert of foulness'. Earlier in the century Madame Vestris, lately of the Lyceum, had leased the theatre for an annual rent of £1,000 and as actress-manageress had made a success of her tenure by spending on redecoration and establishing rules that avoided any irregular escapades back-stage.[5] Her insistence on discipline and her innate good taste brought Madame Vestris a satisfactory return in the manner in which the public applauded her management.

This principle was still alive at the Olympic Theatre when Louisa played her first part there on 12 May 1856 as Mme de Beaupré in *Retribution*. There she found herself in the capable hands of the actor-manager; she would be connected with him and his wife well into the next decade. Alfred Wigan came from an old-established Lancashire family called Wogan until an ancestor having signed the death warrant of Charles I found it propitious to alter the name slightly.[6] Esteemed in the profession – his acting was said to be 'easy, graceful and most true to nature'[7] – educated and well-to-do, 'the only gentleman on the stage – and a worse-dressed one was never seen',[8] Wigan captured, what was more impor-tant, an audience of fashion and discrimination ready to be diverted by burlesque written specially for that much-loved and renowned comedian, Fred Robson, and those short, seemingly amusing comediettas in which the heroine,

The Olympic Theatre, late 1850s

triumphing over vicissitudes of anguish and despair, always won the day. His wife, Leonora, who at the outset had been a rope dancer and performer on stilts, lacked the theatrical accomplishments of her husband but was nevertheless a reliable adjunct to the company, though her affectations, her pretensions to gentility and her well-publicised Court friendships were at singular variance to the start of her career.

By the time Louisa took up work at the Olympic the exterior had been renovated and improvements had been made to the interior. In place of the benched pit, which extended to the orchestra, with its upright bars at intervals optimistically supplying backrests,[9] accommodation had been modified. A semi-circular platform was raised, partly surrounding the pit, to facilitate the movements of the spectator.

[26]

Wigan was soon to introduce stalls at five shillings, the same price as for the dress circle and front boxes, the resort of 'quality'; the pit was from two to three shillings, the gallery at a shilling and the upper gallery at half that price. The institution of 'half-price' at nine o'clock for all parts of the theatre enabled the spectator to see the main piece through to the final curtain at eleven o'clock, all for a reduction in cost.

At the Olympic the stage was moving towards a more naturalistic interpretation. Gone was the sound of the prompter's whistle; the audience no longer saw a sofa and chair being drawn off the stage by a cord while a table was dragged on from the opposite side by the same means.[10] Two chairs no longer indicated that two people were to be seated or their being removed that the two persons were not to be seated.[11] However, certain conventions lingered. The green baize drugget was still spread on the stage portending some tragic act to be committed or a body to fall, warning the audience in advance to prepare itself for an increased thrill of a distressing nature.[12]

Backstage the Green Room, a social essential, was of a respectable size. The dressing rooms, all provided with fireplaces, sinks, water-closets and running water, were divided: two superior rooms above the Green Room and six more, four large and two small, situated below the back part of the pit. The Manager's house in Craven Buildings could supply further accommodation. With the audience dispatched the actors would find their way by midnight to their lodgings or else to various supper rooms in the Strand, Evans's being the most popular. Meanwhile the front of the house would be swathed in brown holland for the night, which would be taken down in the morning when the stage was doused from watering-pots and the company reassembled for rehearsal.

Miss Herbert's first role at the Olympic in Tom Taylor's *Retribution* brought her some acclaim. In her impersonation of Mme de Beaupré *The Era* considered her 'if not a brilliant actress one that would become a useful one in an important walk of the profession'. T. W. Robertson in the *Illustrated Times* was more appreciative:

> I have fallen in love with Mr Wigan's debutante who needs only a little less action with her neck and shoulders to be completely graceful. Were I acquainted with her I should hint that she should drop the 'p' in Baptiste as a French lady would. Miss Herbert is the most hopeful on the London stage, for in her are united great intelligence, much dramatic talent, youth and beauty. Ah! If I were Millais, I would paint her in my next picture in her pure white silk dress, if I were Munro I would carve a lovely medallion from her profile.

Clement Scott, that pre-eminent chronicler of the Victorian theatre, remembered her as 'a lovely girl in the days of the Olympic burlesques and what a hit she made in *Retribution*'. A week after its opening Queen Victoria attended a performance with her husband and son-in-law-to-be, Prince Frederick William of Prussia – the engagement had just been announced. The Princess Royal, ten years younger than her fiancé, was considered too young for a play with its *soupçon* of romantic interest and had been left at home.

Tom Taylor, the author of this melodrama, had written a fine part for a young actress spiced with 'fashionable French'. An earlier play of his, *Still Waters*, had marked a significant break with convention in exposing illicit love as a reality and a fact of life. He was a man of some note – barrister, dramatist, journalist, editor of *Punch* from 1874 to 1880 and in what was known as 'good society', though he was perhaps at his happiest at the Shakespeare Head in Wych Street under Mark Lemon, first editor of *Punch* and known as one of the most 'accomplished humbugs of his time, rude or obsequious by turns as suited his interests'.[13]

Miss Herbert, 'the beautiful Miss Herbert' as she was constantly referred to, was slavishly adored for her looks, her willowy figure, her tresses of golden hair and her grace of movement ('There is no lady on the stage who can enter the room and sit down on the stage as Miss Herbert can'). She had also to endure backstage jealousies, for although it would be fair to say that she would never excel in the higher reaches of her profession, her 'ladylike demeanour' (a phrase often used when describing her performance) and her appearance brought many admirers to the theatre.

Latterly she had established herself in *travesti* parts, in *Alfred the Great* and in the *Doge of Duralto*. *The Era* had commented on the 'more elegant fairy burlesque' in which Miss Herbert took the part of 'Sir Erith Marsh of England, Heir to the Dukedom of Rosherville in Kent' and in a 'glittering dress brought something like prominence' to this susidiary character.

By 1858 she was earning something in the region of £15 a week playing leads, though not rated (financially) a 'star' in professional ability. Sala 'rejoiced at the prosperity of the Olympic' which at its full complement would take £173.

3

Separation and Attachment

Since marriage Louisa and her husband had lived for a year in Onslow Terrace, built in 1824, renting or lodging in one of the eight small houses which, with a cottage, comprised the terrace then on the north west side of the Fulham Road (now the western end of the Brompton Road, the site of St George's Court and Garage). The houses at a half-yearly rate of £2.4.4d could accommodate three persons and a servant and their inhabitants included an attorney's clerk, a master tailor, and a chemist and druggist.

Later the couple moved to 15 Hans Place where their child, Arthur Bingham Crabb, was born on 4 April 1857. Louisa had been out of the theatre for the usual last three months of her pregnancy; it had been a difficult birth and, not having recovered from her confinement, she remained mostly in her room. This was an opportune moment for her husband to seduce Jane, the more than willing chambermaid. There had been trouble earlier with Crabb out all night playing whist, so he said, and now that Louisa was unwell he disappeared for several days without divulging where he had gone. On his return he forbade the servants to attend to her and gave the household keys to the chambermaid. Emma Pottow, Louisa's sister, arrived to care for her and found Crabb closeted with Jane in his dressing-room. Throwing open the door she exclaimed: 'Mr Crabb, I will not allow

Miss Herbert, *by Frederick Sandys, c. 1858*

this, if my sister does.' Jane was sacked by Louisa; Crabb refused to let her leave but left himself, returning only to fetch his clothes. A policeman was called to evict Jane from the house but he refused to interfere.

Louisa communicated with Crabb through her solicitor and a regular deed of separation was executed. It was arranged that he should pay her £25 a quarter on application at Hoare's bank for the maintenance of her son as she was too ill to make an engagement at the theatre. The sum was twice paid and then ceased and Louisa learned that Crabb had gone to India as an indigo planter's assistant and had closed his bank account.

Taking her son with her and adding a final 'e' to the name of Crabb, thus disassociating herself as far as possible from a marriage from which there would be no legal escape, Louisa left Hans Place and for the next three years found shelter at 34 Westbourne Place (now Cliveden Place), a narrow thoroughfare linking Eaton and Sloane Squares, consisting of a neat double row of small houses inhabited by small tradesmen, including an Army clothier and a firm of commercial jewellers. Hers was just large enough for two people and a servant. It was situated suspiciously close to Eaton Place where John Downes Rochfort lived at No. 40 with his mother and sister. Soon to become her lover *en titre*, he was as yet one of her more favoured admirers. Another was Count Limburg-Stirrum and the question circulating the London clubs was which of the two cheeses would win the goddess's fancy – the Limburger, with its characteristic pungent smell when fully ripe and spoiling quickly unless handled carefully, or the Roquefort (Rochfort) which in a class by itself claimed to be the 'fromage des Rois et des Papes'.

John Rochfort was the winner and although she was spectacularly unfaithful to him on one known occasion (also perhaps on others) he was the man Louisa came to love most dearly until the end of his life. Of seemingly unlimited means he was a splendid catch: something of a dasher, of Irish Protestant origin and in some respects strangely strait-laced. His quick temper developed later or perhaps at first the sunshine of his advantages more successfully infused his temperament. He worked as a dedicated and talented amateur artist in pottery decoration and examples of his work show a good deal of skill. Blanks could be acquired, often quite large ones, from manufactures such as Minton and Wedgwood (in Rochfort's case mostly at the Doulton works on Lambeth foreshore) and the artist would decorate these with his own designs and fire them. This was a popular hobby in the second half of the nineteenth century and one of great appeal to Rochfort. By 1860 Doulton's had seventy kilns and Rochfort would do his firing early in the morning.

Born on 7 July 1825, John Rochfort was the only son of his father's second marriage to Mary de Burgh, sister of General Ulysses Baron Downes.[14] The family were descended from De Rochfort of Poitou, an adventurous knight of the twelfth century who when exiled from his own country had been helped, so it was said, by King Henry II, Count of Anjou, to get to Ireland – possibly with the assistance of Pope Adrian IV, the only English Pope. Nearer to our own time 'Prime Iron' Rochfort, a lieutenant-colonel in Cromwell's army, was court-martialled and shot. His son was Speaker of the Irish House of Commons and the Speaker's grandson, Colonel Staunton Rochfort of Clogrenane Castle, Co. Cavan, was the father of our dashing hero. In 1837, when just on fourteen, John Rochfort went to Eton and from there to

Christ Church, Oxford, matriculating in 1842 at the age of nineteen. During the vacations of April and July 1840 he had had two lessons from the artist William Mulready but the twelve guineas owing were not paid until 1843. By 1850 he was a barrister-at-law at Lincoln's Inn but enlisted at Warrington as a lieutenant with the 2nd Royal Lancashire Militia (The Duke of Lancaster's Own Rifles) in April 1853 and was a serving officer based in Liverpool with a once-yearly assembly for four weeks' training until he retired from the Militia in 1862.

The regiment volunteered for foreign service during the Crimean War and embarked in the *Lord Raglan* troopship, reaching Gibraltar in July 1855. The next month Rochfort was raised to the rank of captain. Peace with Russia was signed the following year and the Militia sailed for home on SS *Great Britain*. Rochfort appears to have had no income from his two run-down Irish properties, Bawnboy in Co. Cavan and Lisnagree, Co. Westmeath, but nevertheless lived in style with a household of women at 40 Eaton Place – his widowed mother, his sister Anne, separated from her husband Thomas Blackborne Hildyard, MP, of Flintham Hall, Newark, and Anne's daughter, Edith. Beautiful but dully good, Anne had come upon her husband's letters to his mistress and left him after ten years' marriage. Her sons lived with their father in Eaton Square. At what point Louisa came under the protection of 'Rochey' (as he was called) is not known, though most probably after her escape from Crabb.

4

Stunner No. 1

Louisa was now at the summit of her beauty and she was at last persuaded through the good offices of Tom Taylor to sit to Rossetti. His excitement is apparent in a letter to his friend, the artist William Bell Scott, written while awaiting her arrival at his studio at 14 Chatham Place, Blackfriars, on or about 1 June 1858.

> I am in the stunning position this morning of expecting the actual visit, at ½ past 11, of a model whom I have been longing to paint for years – Miss Herbert of the Olympic Theatre – who has the most varied and highest expression I ever saw in a woman's face, bedsides abundant beauty, golden hair, &c. Did you ever see her? [And after her departure] O my eye she will sit to me for Mary Magdalene in that picture I am beginning. Such luck![15]

A day or two later he reported the event on a visit to G. P. Boyce at his rooms, 15 Buckingham Street, Adelphi. 'He [Rossetti] says she is perfectly beautiful,' Boyce noted in his diary, 'more so even that she looks on the stage.'[16] Louisa, who was of a religious turn of mind, must have relished the image of herself as Mary Magdalene, a reformed prostitute; she was already wearing a golden bauble on a gold chain

[35]

Miss Herbert. Study for the Head of Mary Magdalene
by D. G. Rossetti, 1858

inscribed on its surface 'Noli me tangere' – the perfect badge for the courtesan she had become.

For the next year or more Rossetti made innumerable studies of her, sometimes whole-length reclining in a chair, others of head and shoulders; twice 'from memory'. Her features are captured again in some of his early watercolours, *A Christmas Carol, Mary in the House of St John,* and *Woman in Yellow*. Georgiana Burne-Jones wrote of 'a small water-colour made by Gabriel of her, radiant in golden hair – just the head and throat on an emerald green background and deeply did we feel the tribute rendered to her beauty when we read the names which he had written around the four sides of the little picture: "BEATRICE HELEN GUINEVERE HERBERT".'[17] Ruskin hoped Rossetti might paint her head as the Virgin in his triptych of *The Seed of David* for Llandaff Cathedral. 'I want you to get her beautiful face into your picture as soon as possible.'[18] The painting was started in 1859 and Miss Herbert's image remained on canvas until about 1861 when it was substituted for that of Mrs William Morris.

Other artists immortalised her: Val Prinsep portrayed her on a cigar box dressed in blue wearing a beaver pork-pie hat embellished with a scarlet feather, her golden hair falling to her shoulders. His image of her as *The Queen Was in the Parlour Eating Bread and Honey*, Watts's portrait head in pencil, Frederick Sandys's delicate black chalk whole-length figure, and again, by Sandys, as *Cleopatra Dissolving the Pearl*, drawn in black ink in 1862, Spencer Stanhope's sketch of her for the prostitute in *Thoughts of the Past*,[19] all give adequate expression to the appeal she had for the young artists of the day. Vain and with a strong streak of narcissism, she was very aware of her aesthetic appeal and enjoyed the posing and lounging. Rossetti was among the very few or perhaps the only one who referred to her as 'Ruth' Herbert. James Rennie Swinton, portraitist of the high-born and 'great ladies' of the time,[20] made four portraits of her, though in her most ambitious calculations she can never have seen herself joining the social hierarchy. The smallest of the four was exhibited at the Royal Academy Summer Exhibition of 1859; in the largest she is clad in full shining armour, her sash gathered at the side into a billow of crimson silk while her cloak is thrown back over her shoulders and her hands clasp the heavy hilt of an unsheathed sword. There she stands, in the guise of the Red Cross Knight of Spenser's *Faerie Queen*, embodying in herself one of his twelve moral virtues, that of holiness: The Knight of Holiness, St George of the Red Cross.

It is no surprise that Swinton left no evidence in his account or appointment books of these portraits or that nothing is recorded in well-documented papers of Henry Weigall of the portrait he too made of Louisa; for these were respectable, established artists (no Bohemian hacks, they) and as such should not imperil their positions by letting it be known that they executed commissions to paint what was considered an 'untouchable' in polite Victorian Society, not so much for being an actress (low enough) but for being a kept woman. And commissions they certainly were, executed for Louisa's lovers.

These were the years when Little Holland House acquired a pre-eminence in the artistic and literary world for its 'ambience of fashionable culture'.[21] As dower house to Holland House and set on the confines of the park among ancient trees and seemingly in the depth of the country, this 'rambling and haphazard house' was rented from Lady Holland

Little Holland House, Kensington, *by Emily Prinsep, 1854*

by Thoby Prinsep, director of the East India Company, and for nearly thirty years under Mrs Prinsep's vigilant care it sheltered G. F. Watts from the obligations of mundane life. Here would assemble on warm sunny afternoons the decorative, witty and intellectual elite of the bohemian world of musicians, actors and writers, outstanding among them Browning, Thackeray, Ruskin, Rossetti, Tennyson and Burne-Jones. Over all hung a suggestion of laxity of morals and of ease.

Open house, croquet, bowls on the lawn, crimson chairs and sofas under the trees, a small Persian rug spread on the grass for the men who preferred to lounge at the feet of their adored. Miss Herbert, not over-blessed with all sense of the absurd regarding herself, would in later years when

Miss Herbert, *by D. G. Rossetti, 1858*

Miss Herbert, *by D. G. Rossetti, 1858*

reminiscing with Lady Burne-Jones refer to her visits to Little Holland House to sit to Watts and how the younger men would gather round her and make studies. She had never seen 'such men, it was being in a new world to be with them. I sat to them and was there with them, and they were different to everyone else I ever saw. And I was a holy thing to them – I was a holy thing to them.'[22]

On a June day in 1858 after Louisa had left Little Holland House to prepare for her evening performance at the Olympic Theatre, Rossetti made a drawing of a little scene she had consciously enacted for him that afternoon seated at one of the ground floor windows with a blind half drawn against the sun, coaxing a caged bullfinch. Her features seen in profile are exaggerated: an elongated neck (from memory) supports the head ravishingly framed by the now fashionable smaller bonnet trimmed with chenille bobbles (echoing the familiar pearl earrings seen in most other portraits), the folds of which are gathered softly on the nape of her neck; the frill of embroidered muslin at the throat, the flounced sleeve, the little wrist-length gloves, complete the stunning image to which Rossetti added an inscription:

In Memoriam
25 June 1858

His sonnet, 'Beauty and the Bird' or 'The Bullfinch', written to describe the episode, closes with

Even so, when she, a little lightly red
Now turned on me and laughed, I felt made strong
To honour and to praise her golden head.[23]

He gave the drawing to Georgina Trehearne, a singer of

In Memoriam
25 June 1858

This is a sketch drawn at Little Holland Ho
by Rossetti - Reminiscence of Miss Herbert

Miss Herbert, *by D. G. Rossetti, 1858*

raffish reputation who was herself at Little Holland House that day. On the corner of the drawing she wrote in ink:

> This is a sketch drawn at Little Holland Hse by Rossetti – Reminiscence of Miss Herbert [and an added inscription all but scraped out with a knife] an actress all the Pre-Raffaelites were in love with.

Was it perhaps Miss Herbert herself who in later days of respectability saw to it that the additional words were almost obliterated?

It has recently been claimed[24] that Louisa was Rossetti's mistress. This is without foundation. Miss Herbert was far too busy adroitly negotiating her place in respectability to have any sexual contact with this raffish bohemian. Her ambitions were set on richer material. Her vanity was engaged by his eagerness to draw her but when it came to serious commissioned work she preferred to sit to recognised, gentlemanly artists. Besides which, during the time that Rossetti knew her she was pregnant with a child of one or other of her lovers.

Such was Rossetti's obsession that in this same month of June (1858) he made a watercolour portrait of her on a gold ground, once again 'from memory', glorious in heavy folds of golden hair. In July Louisa had her own Benefit evening at the Olympic, making her appearance in – fitly named – *Going to the Bad*, wearing on stage when first seen a fashionable morning dress of muslin, a bonnet and pink veil and later a rich silk ball dress and white scarf.[25]

Rossetti, fired with his customary zeal in helping a friend in need, invoked the help of Sir John Simon in selling tickets:

> Do you not know [he wrote from Blackfriars] some

lovers of golden hair & the springs of Preraphaelitism who would like to assist at the [performance]? She is a brave girl fighting against grave injustice in & out of the theatre, & greatly needs help, & deserves the best she can get. . . . At any rate it is my duty to try & enlist you, after her great kindness in sitting to me. The tickets are to be got of Miss Herbert, 34 Westbourne Place, Eaton Square.[26]

The day following the Benefit night Rossetti wrote again to thank Sir John for his help. 'It was nearly a "bumper", I am glad to say, and your kind efforts have borne fruit. . . . Let me thank you from Miss Herbert as well as from myself.' He recorded the occasion with a sketch of Louisa seated in the foreground flanked by her male admirers. Her head is lowered over a nosegay, seemingly unaware of the grotesquely ugly man standing before her, his large hands apparently ready to snatch her away. Rossetti inscribed this sketch: 'For the benefit of Miss Herbert July 12 1858.' Probably as a reward for 'her kindness in sitting to me' he gave her the watercolour *Writing on the Sand*, embracing one of the artist's few out-of-doors subjects, and several small sketches besides.

As well as immortalising her in pencil and watercolour Rossetti took some pains to provide her three-year-old son Arthur with a scribbling book, or rather delegated the job to Red Lion Mary, the well-known and much-loved cockney servant at 17 Red Lion Square, High Holborn, where he had had a studio with Deverell. She was now looking after William Morris and Burne-Jones in the same room.

Dear Mary [he wrote] Please go and smash a brute in

Red Lion Passage tomorrow. He had to send a big book – a scrap book, to Master Arthur Crabb

    34 Westbourne Place

    Eaton Square

and he hasn't done it. I dont know his name but his shop is dirty and full of account books. This book was ordered ten days ago and was to have been sent home the next day *and was paid for* – so sit on him hard tomorrow & dig a fork into his eye, as I can't come that way to murder him myself. Yours ever D. G. Rossetti. Please do it though in earnest.[27]

The previous year Louisa had been sitting to W. P. Frith[28] for the lady standing whole-length looking down at her purse in the centre of his large *Derby Day* canvas. She had been suggested to him as being tall, fair and handsome and so he found her to be; but he was unable to capture 'the charm that was before me'. His diary relates how he felt compelled to rub her out and, without telling her, substitute his daughter in her place. Miss Herbert's family had always known a different tale. It was common practice among notable artists to keep open house to their patrons, friends and other artists on Show Sunday, the Sunday before sending in for the Royal Academy Summer Exhibition. On this occasion when the painting was on show in Frith's studio someone exclaimed that the image on the canvas was a libel on Louisa's beauty. Annoyed, Frith took his brush and painted a round hat to conceal the greater part of the face, but everyone knew that it was Miss Herbert. According to Frith, on Louisa's discovery that his daughter was said to have taken her place in the picture she let fly a volley of abusive language (learned perhaps in the stews of Wych Street). It seems unlikely that the artist would have repainted the entire figure and why obliterate his daughter's face with a hat? The figure as it stands in its flounced, sprigged muslin dress is probably Miss Herbert's; the hat shades the face in anonymity. The fact that the *Athenaeum* of 1 May 1858, reviewing the painting, paid scant attention to this central figure while writing in detail of the composition and its components was perhaps a safeguard in avoiding any argument.

5

'The Chaste Dian'

The Divorce Bill had become law at the end of 1857, though such were the difficulties of 'unriveting the *vincula matrimonii*' and so formidable the amount of pay as to make the Act 'virtually a dead letter to the poor man'.[29] Besides, the scandal of divorce would doom any woman in the eyes of Society. There was little differentiation in the mind of the public between an actress and a prostitute; 'actress' was still a disreputable description while at the police courts it was but a polite euphemism for a 'tart';[30] so it must have been with some consternation that Miss Herbert found herself pregnant in September while playing in *Ticklish Times* (so apt were the titles to fit her circumstances) and withdrew from the cast at the end of the year.

Louisa's situation at this juncture was a critical one. It was imperative for Rochfort's sake, the father of the child, that he should not suffer malicious innuendoes because of her, for while it was quite in accordance with the double standards of morality for him to keep a mistress, he must not flaunt her openly. The birth was in May 1859 and since it was unacceptable for Rochfort to acknowledge the parentage, the boy when baptised in January 1861 at Old St Pancras Church (a church not unfamiliar with irregular births) was christened Cecil Bayley, the last name, probably that of the mid-wife, thereafter constituting his surname. The parents were declared to be Edward and Louisa Crabbe residing in Hunter Street, presumably for a limited night or two – if at all – to provide an obscure address. There was not much likelihood of detection as those christened at the same time were children of waiters, labourers and of those living in the workhouse.

Louisa was back at the Olympic at the beginning of 1860 playing a variety of roles, drawing an audience if not by her professional skills then by her ability to establish herself as foremost in the refinements of 'ladylike' parts. This was a time when an aura of respecatability was creeping in and a new school of drama where the naturalistic technique of which T. W. Robertson was the exponent that purported to hold up a mirror to life, was in the ascendant.[31]

The spring of 1860 saw the revival of the Volunteer movement formed in fear of Louis Napoleon. The Artists' Rifle Corps in which Ruskin was 'Honorary Member' was joined by Millais, Morris, Rossetti, Prinsep, Swinburne and others. Rossetti's assistance was of the shortest: on being told to turn right he would question 'Why?', and Morris under the same instructions would invariably turn left and then apologise to the man facing him. Tom Taylor was in the Whitehall Company; W. S. Gilbert in the one of Somerset House. The Government had two Post Office companies on the strength in one of which Edmund Yates, novelist, journalist, dramatic critic, served as ensign to his commander, Hubert Harrington, a colleague in the Post Office and collaborator in dramatic work. Heavily built with a fund of good humour, Yates nevertheless made enemies with his sharp tongue. It was said that he wrote with a red hot poker but he was a great figure in the world of the theatre, a son of actors. Drills, field days and inspections took place in the spring in preparation for 22 June when Queen Victoria was to review 21,000 Volunteers in Hyde Park. In the previous April Yates, writing to Miss Herbert on 'April 19/60', conjured her to be at her window:

> Loveliest of your sex & goddess of the P.R.B.! If you would behold the flower of the manly youth of the land, be at your window about 3 on Saturday and behold the march of the Civil Service Brigade. Your devoted slave (for self & Harrington)
>
> EDMUND YATES [32]

During the summer while acting in *Dearest Mama*, a comedietta adapted from the French, Louisa's own mother died in Bristol at the age of sixty-eight, having suffered for four years from '*ramolissement*'[33] of the brain, and certified. Fanny Maynard had never recovered from the shock of the loss of her son at sea and would walk the streets of Bristol stopping strangers, enquiring of them whether they knew his whereabouts. Her husband, still living at Limehouse, was with her when she died at her daughter Emma's house in Lower Maudlin Street where the Pottows' lucrative trade was carried on. On her death certificate John Maynard was still calling himself a brassfounder as well as the new attribution of 'journeyman', denoting some kind of qualification which set him above a common labourer. Furthermore, unable to sign his name he made his mark with a cross; he was known to suffer dreadfully from rheumatism and could hardly have been illiterate.

The Olympic Theatre under Wigan's management had brought Miss Herbert success and a certain independence and when in September 1860 he took over the St James's Theatre as its lessee he offered her the female lead in his new

The St James's Theatre, 1870s

company, which included the sixteen-year-old Kate Terry
(Ellen's elder sister) and her father. This was heady stuff for
Louisa. The theatre (pulled down in 1957) stood on the site
of the tumbledown Nevot's Hotel in King Street, facing
Christie's. The stage door opened onto Angel Court, a
roofed-over passageway running down the side of the theatre
towards Pall Mall. Built for John Bramham, distinguished
tenor and father of Frances Lady Waldegrave, it had opened
in December 1835 and was said to be 'the most splendid in
Europe'. It had never flourished, although in the early 1850s,

''ere the efflorescence of the beautiful Miss Herbert',[34] the St James's Theatre had held several interesting seasons of French plays in which the celebrated Rachel had shone as Phèdre and in others of her great roles; and this had often brought Queen Victoria to the theatre. It was redecorated in 1859, and Wigan, on taking up the management, raised the prices, though keeping the gallery at sixpence, and restored the second-price seats.

Louisa was now to enter her most effective years on the stage even if Ellen Terry, while observing that Miss Herbert 'looked like the Blessed Damosel leaning out "across the bar of heaven"', did not think her well suited to the parts she was playing.[35] She opened in October 1860 in Tom Taylor's *Up at the Hills*, as Mrs Eversleigh, in a drama of Anglo-Indian life. The 'Dramatic Lounger' of the *Illustrated Times* (27 October 1860) reported: 'If it be a true picture of English life at a station on the Neilgherries morals there are in a very slack condition.' Mrs Eversleigh's golden hair, very much to the fore, elicited from an admirer: 'I don't wonder the flies are caught in this golden web', and – more prosaically spoken by a Mrs Colonel McCann to Mrs Eversleigh – 'Is he to be the next eaten, you insatiable little spider?' This was hugely successful particularly when such words as 'tiffin' and a 'peg' of soda and brandy were introduced (rather 'fast', that) and the Anglo-Indian newly arrived greenhorn was referred to as a 'griff'.

Two Christmas pieces filled the bill at the end of the year, a classical mythological extravagance, *Endymion*, in which Miss Herbert played 'Diana the Goddess of Hunting, otherwise known as Luna or the Moon, in all respects a shining character'. A daughter of Lord Stratford de Redcliffe made two sketches of her in the part; in the one 'an upstanding silver crescent in her very golden hair and a blue chiton, tight in the wrong places as a concession to the classical ideal',[36] the other in watercolour, head and shoulders, uniquely wearing make-up. The length of neck is emphasised, a bandeau twined around her head, a crescent moon surmounting it. She was remembered as 'that superb creature whose name conjures up old memories of the Strand and the Olympic and the never forgotten image of chaste Dian's descent upon the crescent of the moon to her beloved'.[37] Among the young nymphs were Kate Terry and the equally youthful Nelly Moore who would later captivate Henry Irving.

The other Christmas offering was a melodrama adapted from the French by Frank Burnand, reduced from six acts to four and renamed the *Isle of St Tropez*. A Roman Catholic, Burnand (later Sir Francis) when a very young man had received instruction for the priesthood, but finding himself unsuited settled for play-writing and journalism instead. Wigan played opposite Miss Herbert and Mrs Wigan directed. Kate Terry was in the cast as was her father, Ben Terry, in a small part. Not long after the opening Sir Walter and Lady Trevelyan, of Wallington, Northumberland, were in the audience; she noted in her diary that the melodrama was 'a clever thing and interesting. Mr Wigan very good. Stunner Herbert looked quite ugly as the heroine, the headdress so utterly misbecame her.' However, they were much pleased 'on the whole'.[38] This ran till the end of the season but by mid-March Louisa's voice seems to have lost its attraction: a playbill of that time has a note against her name by a member of the audience, pronouncing her 'coarse voiced'. The season ended in May 1861 but *Endymion* had its last performance in March. This may have been owing to the chiton – 'tight in the wrong places' and all too-revealing, for Louisa, 'the chaste Dian', was again pregnant.

Miss Herbert had moved from Westbourne Place and by early 1861 had established herself on the south side of Piccadilly at No. 193, premises belonging to the publishers Chapman & Hall. Her immediate neighbours were a tobacconist at 191, six houses beyond Hatchards; a police constable at 192 and on her other side, Jones the Butcher. She was now within much easier reach of St James's Theatre.

The 1861 census gives her name as Louisa Crabb (the final 'e' not legally adopted); head of household, of no occupation and her age as twenty-six. (Six years earlier she had marked up twenty-four years on her marriage certificate.) Young Arthur Crabb (no mention of the two-year-old Cecil Bayley), a housemaid, a cook and a lady's maid (probably her dresser) completed the household.

However, for the birth of the new arrival Louisa resorted to 4 Pelham Villas (now the site of South Kensington Underground Station) where a daughter was born in August 1861. The father, a friend of Rochfort, was the handsome, wealthy, debonair and urbane rake, Frederick Acclom Milbank, of an old-established Yorkshire family. Married, with two sons, he had inherited much of his fortune from his grandfather, the 1st Duke of Cleveland. Liberal in manner and outlook, a thorough *bon vivant*, lover of the arts and a patron of the drama, he was a Member for the North Riding of Yorkshire for twenty years from 1865 and was created a baronet in 1882. 'Fred the Rip', as he was known, was a famous gun and rented a castle every year in the Outer Hebrides for several months and once shot 190 grouse in a twenty-minute drive. Besides sharing Louisa, he and Rochfort shared a collector's voracious appetite; Milbank's in

Miss Herbert, 1860

particular was for old silver and he was known to be a reckless bidder at Christie's.

A Sarah Bayley, presumably the midwife who had given her name to Louisa's earlier bastard, registered the child's birth, giving the father's name as Edward Crabb, a 'gentleman' – this was safe with Crabb in India planting and cutting down indigo – and the baby's name as Madeline Augusta. An 'e' was inserted later giving the frenchified look of 'Madeleine' – just as well, as in 1871, living at another address and on purpose to mystify, the child was simply called Augusta Crabbe in the public census, born in Paris and niece of Louisa. A note of fantasy is struck when fifteen months after Midge (as she was always called) was born, the father made her a financial settlement quoting her name as 'Magdalene'. At that time there were Magdalene Houses in plenty for the reform of prostitutes, perhaps a frivolous jest in which father and mother participated.

6

Bold, Bad, Fascinating Lady Audley

The season opened again in the late autumn (1861) and by the end of the year George Vining had taken over as manager and leading man in the place of Wigan. This was a man who whenever criticised brought an action for libel: 'one of the most sensitive and litigious actors that ever lived'.[39] His voice was of the rasping variety and he thought highly of his own competence as an actor. Milbank was the lessee of the theatre, presumably underwriting any losses, thus ensuring that the theatre which in the past had suffered many reversals should remain solvent and that Miss Herbert would carry out the leading roles. In the spring of 1862 she had been indisposed and at short notice Kate Terry, barely eighteen, had taken over her part in *Friends and Foes*, a translation from Sardou's *Nos Intimes*; a deserved opportunity as she had studied every part and she was rewarded by making her first great hit.

On July 1862 both *The Athenaeum* and *The Era* reported a 'pretty quarrel' arising between Vining, Miss Herbert, Milbank, and Watts Phillips, dramatist and journalist, pupil of Cruikshank and an early contributor to *Punch* and now the author of *His Last Victory*, 'my little Drama', which had been suddenly removed from the bill at the St James's Theatre after barely a week's run while he was in Paris. Vining had written to him confidentially that this was to happen,

Frederick Acclom Milbank, *by Frederick Sandys, 1872*

accusing Miss Herbert who was playing the lead of not caring for the play. Letters to the public were printed in *The Athenaeum*: from Watts Phillips to the effect that the piece had been taken out of the bill 'to gratify the caprice of a lady', to which Miss Herbert (signing herself 'Ruth Herbert') replied that his letter was 'a tissue of falsehoods from beginning to end'. Frederick Milbank then took the field as lessee of the theatre. He alone was responsible for having withdrawn the play 'owing to its being, in my opinion, as poor a Drama as ever was produced on the stage'. Both the dramatist and Vining had more to tell the public but the sparring was no more than a brush with untoward pressures of theatre life and made little impact. Watts Phillips became a friend of Milbank and a very great admirer of Miss Herbert, who was perhaps a trifle wearied by his devotion. By 1869 he was writing to the eight-year-old Midge, sending messages through her to her mother. The letters carry delightful drawings such as to amuse a child and are signed 'Watch Phillips', as presumably pronounced by her.

Recovering from the slight contretemps of early July, on the 19th of that month Miss Herbert had a stall at the Dramatic Fête held annually at the Crystal Palace, Sydenham, entrance fee 2s 6d. One of the visitors found it remarkable that 'actresses, charming on the stage, are mere simpering dummies off'; he found few were able to make conversation to tempt people to buy their wares. Miss Herbert especially came in for adverse comment, for 'possessed of a singularly handsome face, and capable of posing to perfection, [she] has no conversational power when placed behind the stall'.[40] This corroborates an observation that the 'conversational stock of actresses is painfully limited and strictly circumscribed by the narrow horizon of self'.[41] Poor Louisa, anxious as always to preserve her dignity as a 'lady', 'polished by the most emotional of all arts', clung to the belief that though all leading dramatic heroines did not 'become the wives of baronets', nevertheless the practice of their calling so refined and educated their sentiments that they were always ladies.[42]

Although all parties remained on friendly terms, if there had ever been a rift between Louisa and John Rochfort owing to the introduction of Midge, there appears to have been a reconciliation in September. Rochfort gave her two books: the one, *Crabbe's Poetical Works*, he inscribed, with the date, to 'Louisa Crabbe' (did she, with the additional 'e' at the end of her married name, claim through her generally unknown husband, some unfounded connection with the poet?), and the second book, Homer's *Iliad*, translated by Pope, is inscribed simply with her Christian names and again the date. Pages of verse much underscored, 'What winning graces! What majestic mien! She moves a goddess, and she looks a queen' must have found a ready acceptance in the recipient's breast.

At the Theatre Royal, Westminster (Astley's of earlier days), Tom Taylor's comic drama *To Parents and Guardians*, in which Miss Herbert took a leading role, opened three nights before Christmas, but she was back at the St James's at the New Year (1863), where Frank Matthews was Manager, G. C. Ellis stage manager and Willliam Beverley the eminent scene painter. She herself played a variety of parts until on 28 February she made a striking success in *Lady Audley's Secret*, a dramatised version of Miss Braddon's sensational novel of the previous year. This is a tale of supposed murder where Lady Audley pushes her husband, a decent man without money, down a well and marries a rich and noble one whose family she handles with the utmost skill. But there had been a witness to her foul deed so she set fire to the inn to kill the one person who could incriminate her. With the reappearance of her first husband – not drowned in the well – and finding herself a bigamist, Lady Audley goes mad and with a wild laugh falls and dies 'to a tableau of sympathy'. No wonder the production ran for a hundred nights followed by a provincial tour. 'Bold, bad, fascinating' Lady Audley was a fine part for Miss Herbert, full of histrionics which she encompassed triumphantly.

Every anticipation, however sanguine, was fully realised in the amount of 'intellectual power Miss Herbert bestowed upon the impersonation of a guilty woman prompted to crime by a hereditary insanity', which was seized upon and acclaimed as 'exquisitely true'. She made a profound impression on the crowded house on the first night and for all the richness of melodramatic incident the audience, having a 'pudding all plums', remained insatiable.

Miss Braddon wrote a generous letter to the heroine expressing her delight in Miss Herbert's 'grace and self possession. Your charmingly distinct articulation and ever-varying expression of your face.' She felt that in the 'last wild shriek of mingled madness and despair at the end' the actress was 'inimitable'. This was one of Miss Herbert's most famous roles but it was not free from criticism and professional jealousy which no doubt led Kate Bateman, ten years younger and then acting in *Leah* at the Adelphi, to write to Augustus Daly in August describing the performance: 'She had a way of rushing down to the footlights, thrusting her head very far out and winking one eye – which was truly splendid! I shall try in the third act of *Leah* and I am sure it will at any rate astonish the audience.'[43]

At the end of the summer season and with the play's success behind her, Miss Herbert went with the company on tour to the provinces. At Bristol on 15 September the *Western Daily Press* described her as 'a lady who is a native, we believe, of this city, and one of the most shining lights to the profession which Bristol has produced'. This was her return to the Theatre Royal, built in 1766, modelled on Drury Lane, where in 1854 she had rather ignominiously appeared under the auspices of James Doughty and his Performing Dogs.

Earlier however, in March, another of Miss Braddon's novels had been dramatised and performed at the Princess's Theatre. Writing to Miss Herbert, the novelist lamented how 'sadly we wanted Mr Milbank' to play one of the two male leads in *Aurora Floyd*. She hoped that 'your houses still continue crowded and that you will have all the peerage in your private boxes'. Lord Ernest Bruce, that very early and long-standing admirer, would most certainly have been among them.

The year 1863 had been an exciting one for Louisa. Not only had she achieved a triumph in demonstrating that she could accomplish something beyond burlesque but her ambition was now directed to the management of the theatre itself (with the assistance of a certain Yorkshire purse). Meanwhile Rochfort, sealing their affection with something more than words, financial support and fatherhood, bought a house in to which he settled Louisa with her covey of three young children, Arthur Crabbe, Cecil Bayley and Midge (Crabbe).

As you turned down from the Old Brompton Road, Sidmouth Lodge, on the east side of The Boltons, looked south towards facing crescents which in the middle embraced St Mary's Church. The house was built in 1838 and derived its name from the son of the first occupant who had been born

Sidmouth Lodge, The Boltons

there. Still very much in the country and close to what had
been until recently a cherry orchard, this charming, quite
large, detached villa, Greek Revival in style, on two floors
with a small cottage to one side, was well set back in a large
garden with pleasant trees within a low surrounding wall.
The heavy gate between stone posts opened on to Gilston
Road; once inside, the carriage sweep carried to the 'grave
and narrow entrance between Ionic columns'[44] rising to the
height of the frieze which in turn supported a stone panel
enriched with bas-reliefs. A note exists[45] for a room to be
decorated in 1864 by Alexander Cowan & Sons, papermaker
of 77 Cannon Street, London E.C., with instructions to 'strip
the walls, supply and put up Flock papers & borders & paint
ditto. Pick out cornice. For Sidmouth Lodge, Old Brompton',
the order being placed by 'Rochfort, Eaton Place'. A sample
of the paper shows a small rather undistinguished sage green
pattern on an ivory ground.

John Rochfort continued to live at his mother's house in Eaton Place to keep up appearances and for the sake of decorum which she would have required – a gentleman openly consorting with an actress was not welcome in Society. Thankfully, although an artist he was an amateur artist, which absolved him from gross transgression of Victorian respectability, for artists were scarcely acceptable in that world where each one knew his place and kept to it. 'At a time . . . when an artist and a gentleman were terms held to be antipodean',[46] Rochey, 'a man of leisure who adopted pottery purely as a recreation . . . who did good work',[47] practised it with enthusiasm and it was of some quality. Vases, chargers, cisterns, all of varying dimensions but mostly of some size and highly decorated, even tiles for a washstand, were executed in the 1860s. He spent liberally at auction on his own collections of ceramics, two della Robbia plaques, a sixteenth-century dish; clocks, silver-gilt cups, a bronze group, shrines, Byzantine enamels, all appear as acquisitions illustrated in watercolour in his small sketch books. In February 1862 he copied a Rossetti drawing of Miss Herbert onto a large circular dish, painting her image in the centre framed by a circle of winged *putti* rapturously enclosing her in a garland of pink roses. A twisting ribbon proclaims her 'Luisa Bella' and adds the date '1862'. At the base of the black, yellow-decorated border, her initials 'L C' form a decorative motif within a shield, while placed at the top is a concocted coat of arms.

A *carte de visite* photograph of Rochfort taken in the early part of the 1860s shows a man of some height, perhaps six foot, with a high domed forehead, receding hair and side whiskers, leaning nonchalantly against bookshelves lined with bound volumes of periodicals. He is smartly dressed if

John Downes Rochfort, c.1861

somewhat eccentric, in a long frock coat with top hat at his side. Here is a man at ease with himself.

The management of the St James's Theatre changed hands at the end of 1863. Frank Matthews had not been well and had unexpectedly asked Ben Webster of the Adelphi Theatre to take over. This Webster was prepared to do, bringing his own company with him while Frederick Milbank stood in for a few weeks to enable him to make his arrangements. In April 1864 Miss Herbert was engaged as Lady Elizabeth Freelove in a revival of an old farce, *The Day after the Wedding. Tallis* commented that she had 'perhaps the best stage appearance of any English actress, however meagre her other qualities may be'. Notwithstanding her lack of skill 'the theatre was crowded with rank and fashion' and this was of enormous importance to Louisa. Having so resolutely cultivated the refinements of elegance and taste and having acquired a certain distinction of manner (though her diction is rarely mentioned, nor any technical ability), by watching and studying and by keeping her origin scrupulously in the shadows, she carried off aristocratic parts, in adopting the style of one who had lived perhaps on the fringes of privilege.

Louisa's elder sister, Jane, at the somewhat advanced age of nearing forty, married William Rickards Tenniel, son of John Baptist Tenniel and brother of John Tenniel the well-known black and white illustrator. The groom gave his occupation as 'artist'. His father was witness at his wedding on 21 July 1864 at St James's Church, Paddington, but the marriage was not popular with his family and John Tenniel's observation in September about 'the late trouble and anxiety'[48] having been too much for his mother may well have referred to this ill-assorted match. A Tenniel daughter had married Leopold, son of John Martin the painter and godson of Prince Leopold, but the eldest son was giving them nothing to celebrate by connecting himself with a close-on middle-aged daughter of a brass foundry labourer (though classified by now a 'gentleman' on the marriage certificate), with a sister-in-law thrown in who was both an actress and mother of two illegitimate children. William Tenniel had succumbed to the overriding influence of an exacting father who had taught him among other particulars, such as fencing and boxing, the waltz at Almack's and insisted on his becoming an instructor of the dance.[49] For a while the couple lived at Delamere Cresecent, Maida Vale, not far from others of the Tenniel family, Jane constantly asking her sister for money. Two daughters were born, Minnie and Jessie, who were sent to school eventually in Dresden where they were known as the 'two English princesses' for their pink and white complexion, blue eyes, long golden hair and graceful carriage no doubt taught them by their father. Minnie, the elder of the two, always maintained that as a child she had been her Uncle John's model for Alice in *Through the Looking Glass*.

7

The Manageress

When Miss Herbert at last came into her kingdom as Manageress of the St James's Theatre in December 1864 ('in real or nominal management' as was said) she received an exceptionally warm welcome from the public.

> The directress of the new venture at the St James's Theatre is Miss Herbert, a graceful sympathetic person of much beauty with exquisite golden hair and almost devotional features who supplied many of the PreRaphaelite Brethren with angelic faces for their canvases. On the stage her efforts were directed by much sympathy and spirit and she was now about to essay the difficulties and perplexities of management.

The theatre opened on Boxing Day, 1864, with Miss Herbert in the part of Omphale in *Hercules and Omphale*, a burlesque by William Brough. Her impersonation was reported to have been 'characterised by all that classic grace expression and pose that has achieved for her a position in burlesque, unique and unrivalled'. But burlesque demanded dancing on the part of the principal and (at the age of thirty-three) 'the stately Miss Herbert dances, but thank heaven! it is not a double shuffle. And so thank heaven – and her own good taste – Miss Herbert did not dance the hornpipe! She danced instead the prettiest of Grecian minuets.'[50]

In February another comedy followed, *Faces in the Fire*, witnessed by Lewis Carroll who thought the actress 'very clever'.[51] *The Era* observed that 'she threw into her impersonation all those graces of refinement and intelligence which lend such a fascinating influence to all the characters the lady embodies.'

The season ended with the inevitable Benefit for Miss Herbert but not before she had scored a further success in *Eleanor's Victory*, another adaptation from a novel by Miss Braddon (whose name was misspelt on the playbill). She was in the box on the first night but was unfortunately ignored in favour of the applause and cries for Miss Herbert between the acts and at the final curtain when she received a rapturous ovation. A playgoer noted approvingly on a playbill under her name: 'sans crinoline'.

In reviewing *Caught in the Toils*, the play which opened the season in December, the 'Dramatic Lounger' (rightly Tom Robertson), theatre critic of the *Illustrated Times*, admired Miss Herbert's performance in the part of Julia where 'she exercised power with all the fascination of the boa and the spring of the cobra, polished and deadly as an oiled rifle-bullet', but the sooner an author found a part 'worthy of her great abilities' the better. It failed to attract and was replaced first by *Lady Audley's Secret* and towards the end of the year by *St James's Ladies Club*.

Frank Matthews was back at the theatre, as was his wife, old friends now; so too was Charles Mathews whose Sunday dinners at 25 Pelham Crescent were celebrated – he, now the most perfect artist on the stage, in his smoking cap, dressing-gown and slippers and Mrs Charley his second wife, 'the queen of hostesses', who from having been a very handsome dark-haired woman had become a brilliant blonde.[52] Buckstone, Ben Webster, the seventy-year-old Planché, Palgrave Simpson, Miss Herbert, Yates and in a year or two Henry Irving, and many others were among the convivial group. On alternate Sundays the Frank Matthewses would entertain in their own house, Linden Grove, Notting Hill. In years to come Clement Scott and Miss Herbert would recall, with the 'assistance of the bright memory of Mrs Charley', the many old associations.[53]

During the autumn Ben Webster had sent Miss Herbert the dramatised version of Miss Braddon's novel *East Lynne* (1861), suggesting that she might care to produce it at the St James's. She replied from Sidmouth Lodge on 14 November 1865:

> My dear Sir, I have read your play of East Lynne and like some parts of it very much. On the whole I fear it is too sad – and now I am determined to bring out no more plays founded on novels. I dont believe they satisfy the public. I regret that I have pledged myself to produce another play from a novel at Xmas. I am at the same time extremely obliged to you for allowing me to see your manuscript.[54]

Louisa seems to have extricated herself from her undertaking to stage another dramatisation, unless she simply postponed Ouida's novel *Idalia* until 1867, as the year ended with *The School for Scandal* ('a radiantly lovely Lady Teazle'). It was the fashion to offer a full bill packed with curtain-raisers and afterpieces but Miss Herbert gained good marks by giving only one or other of these with the main piece as her 'sole sop to fashion'. With Sheridan's *The School for Scandal* in the bill for Boxing Day she added *Please to Remember the Grotto, or The Manageress in a Fix.* Encouraged by the decided hit she had made as Lady Teazle she decided to revive the classics and in the first half of 1866 Goldsmith, Sheridan and Shakespeare were foremost. When he was reviewing a performance of *The School for Scandal* on 3 March, a note of asperity entered the Dramatic Lounger's usually glowing tribute. The Prince of Wales had exercised his prerogative as a friend, or at least his influence, to have the Manageress change the bill to suit him on the previous Monday and to perform Sheridan's play instead of Goldsmith's *She Stoops to Conquer.* The critic found the scenery seedy and the dresses an anachronism. Management was exonerated when on 17 March the Prince and Princess of Wales attended a performance of *She Stoops to Conquer* where Miss Herbert 'with ladylike grace' played Kate Hardcastle.

At a time when ritualism in Anglican churches was fast gaining ground, *Punch* was quick to satirise the clergy's eagerness to wear vestments and adorn their church furnishings, advising them of the wisdom to do the thing well by applying to Miss Herbert, playing Beatrice in *Much Ado about Nothing* 'at the St James's Theatre (a saint's theatre too!) who had got a properly vested altar, including two candlesticks, which was used as a property and we have no doubt ample use will be found for it in the latest Ecclesiastical drama, which, by the way, might very appropriately adopt the above-mentioned Shakespearean title.'[55]

Louisa's Beatrice, according to the *Illustrated Times*, 'to borrow an Americanism, is "real grist"'; and 'as played by Miss Herbert is the sort of noble brilliant woman to inspire any man with a true love and it occurred to me that Prince

Pedro [Walter Lacy] is thoroughly in earnest when he says "Will you have me, lady?"' It was hoped that for the future Miss Herbert would confine herself to high comedy and not attempt melodrama again, 'for melodrama is for artistes of an inferior grade'.

The St James's Theatre had never been an exceptionally lucky one and the last few years had not added to its fortunes. Miss Herbert may have been an attraction of a sort, but the majority of her performances had been in plays of no obvious merit. That she had turned to the classics was a wise decision but a fortuitous alternative to her plans brought Henry Irving into her theatre.

8

Henry Irving

In 1866 Henry Irving joined Miss Herbert's company at the St James's Theatre. He was born in Somerset in 1838 from a simple farming-stock background. His father had led a precarious life as travelling salesman to the village general store. As a young man the father had sought his fortune unsuccessfully in Bristol where his brother who accompanied him did well for himself with a firm of iron merchants. This was in the late 1820s and he could have been an acquaintance of John Maynard – though it is unlikely that Louisa ever investigated the possible contingency.

Irving had determined at an early age and with a singleness of mind to be an actor. His first step was to change his name from Brodribb to Irving, having admired the evangelical preacher Edward Irving and enjoyed the tales of Washington Irving as a boy. Poor and almost unknown, he found provisional work as a 'walking on gentleman' in Sunderland's Royal Lyceum stock company and for two and a half years at thirty shillings a week he took juvenile leads at the Theatre Royal, Edinburgh. An ignominious engagement at the Princess's Theatre, London, under Augustus Harris's management, sent him back to the provinces in 1860 to gain some measure of recognition at Manchester. He would take anything, whatever the type of play or character to be performed or wherever an opening offered: Bury, Oxford,

Birmingham, a long and thankless grind sometimes at a guinea a week. At Liverpool he was more successful, playing in farce and burlesque. Here in his late twenties, still in despairing poverty, he received a letter from Dion Boucicault in Manchester in 1866, offering him a part in a play of his own, *The Two Lives of Mary Leigh*, at the Prince's Theatre, in which Kate Terry was to play the heroine and Irving Rawdon Scudamore, the male lead. He lost no time in presenting himself.

The play opened on 30 July 1866 and was roundly trounced by the critics though Irving won acclaim for his performance. Charles Reade, sensing that the play would be successful in London and admiring the actor's performance, offered Boucicault a London production. Although a friend, but having an eye to a more lucrative opportunity, Boucicault managed a better deal with Miss Herbert, advising her to take it. Dion Boucicault, Irish actor and dramatist, hard-working and conscientious, was known as a 'diamond to cut a diamond'[56]; if there could only be one winner, he made sure it was he.

Miss Herbert was eager to play the part of Mary Leigh; the only condition imposed was that Irving should play Scudamore and at £3 a week. Rehearsals began in September, the title of the play having been changed to *Hunted Down*. Irving was not only acting the male lead, he had also been engaged as stage manager. In an unfamiliar London theatre and among actors he did not know rehearsals were slower than expected and the opening was postponed from early October for a month. In the search for a stopgap, *The Belle's Stratagem* was produced, in which Irving as Doricourt was scarcely noticed though Miss Herbert (Letitia Hardy) 'added another success to the list of her many professional triumphs'; she was encored in the song 'Where are you going to, my pretty maid?'

On the evening of 5 November 1866 the curtain of the St James's rose to a distinguished audience; when it fell Henry Irving's reputation had been made that night. The three-act drama centred on blackmail and bigamy, Irving playing the villain, Miss Herbert the ill-used heroine (Mary Leigh) who triumphed at the close. Turning to leave her box after the tumultuous applause, George Eliot asked G. H. Lewes what he thought of Irving's performance. 'In twenty years', replied Lewes, 'he will be at the head of the English stage.' 'He is there, I think, already,' replied the novelist.[57]

Meanwhile, Louisa had asked Tom Robertson if he would write her something as a Christmas piece, but too busy himself he suggested W. S. Gilbert, a young barrister and witty conversationalist. *Dulcamara! or The Little Duck and the Great Quack* was the happy result. Within ten days he had written what he called 'an eccentricity', a skit on Donizetti's *L' Elisir d'Amore*, his first piece for a professional theatre. Showing more attention to enunciation, for he insisted that every syllable should be heard and never slurred, he had not discussed what sum of money he would receive for his burlesque, so that when after the success of the first night W. Emden, acting manager, inquired of him his terms, Gilbert, fearing that a round sum in pounds might give the impression that he was not an *homme du monde*, asked modestly, for thirty guineas. Emden seemed surprised and a shade disappointed. 'We never pay in guineas, Mr Gilbert. Make it pounds.' 'Done!' said Gilbert. Then handing him the cheque, Emden offered some advice: 'Never sell so good a piece as this for £30 again.'[58]

Louise de la Ramée, known more familiarly to the public

as Ouida, the young and very popular novelist, had had her
novel *Idalia* adapted for the stage. '*Idalia* is about to be
dramatised', she wrote, 'with the loveliest of English actresses
in the role of Idalia.'[59] Intolerably spoilt by her celebrity,
arrogant and vain, she was delighted to see her work on the
stage, for the character she had shaped as Idalia was the
apotheosis of Ouida herself. The plot, set during the 1859
struggle for Italian independence, an episode which held the
sympathy of the British public and was still relatively fresh in
the memory, was slightly altered from the novel and much
suited to Miss Herbert's inclination towards the *haut monde*.
Here as Countess Idalia – albeit a spy and a beautiful one –
she has as her fellow conspirator Count Falcon (Irving) who
in melodramatic fashion turns out to be her long-lost father.
Romantic scenes took place on Lago di Garda and the Piazza
del Duomo at Brescia was alight with the red glare of bonfires
on the eve of the Battle of Solferino. But on the first night
(April 1867) the unpredictable occurred. It had been a particularly cold early spring with water freezing and ice and
snow lingering until April. In Scene 2 of *Idalia*[60] a real water-
fall splashed down from a high point in the backcloth, sup-
posedly to run under a bridge and off stage. Instead, too
much water came tumbling down on and over the sides of
the bridge and downstage and as it spread it froze. Unaware
of the circumstances under which the first member of the cast
to enter had slipped and taken a tumble, Irving, the spy, in
making a stealthy appearance on to the bridge had lost his
footing within seconds, shot into the air and slithered down
to the footlights 'to the delight of the spectators now all agog
for the next victim'. This was Charles Wyndham (almost his
London professional début); he had peeped to see the cause
of the laughter and had managed to avoid an icy fall but

Miss Herbert, unprepared for what lay in wait, immediately slipped and lost her balance 'so that she fell, spread-eagled, her voluminous skirts and petticoats swirling up so that all the hysterical audience could see were her lovely long legs convulsively kicking'.

The next scenes brought more trouble. Although carpets had been spread they were not large enough to cover some remaining ice patches and Miss Herbert and Wyndham with outflung arms were thrown up and then went down to 'slither forward on their bottoms; never had an audience at the St James's enjoyed themselves so much'. By the time the last scene was reached it was not only they but the players as well who were holding their sides with laughter and finally the whole company joined in merriment with the audience.

That summer of 1867 Miss Herbert took her company on a successful provincial tour. In Manchester in August *The School for Scandal* received good notices, Louisa affording 'a glimpse of those far higher artistic qualities of which few even of her admirers have any definite knowledge'. Dublin saw her as Lydia Languish in *The Rivals* in a role she had sustained in London 'with a sentiment and delicacy which imparts much grace to the performance'.

Following their summer tour Irving had undertaken a private engagement as star performer at the Prince of Wales's Theatre, Liverpool. It fell to G. C. Ellis, who had assumed the function of stage manager, to remind him that rehearsals for the autumn would start on 7 October. To this Irving replied:

You surely know that my engagement with Mr Henderson extends beyond this week. I regret that I cannot be with you on the 7th – it is quite impossible – my word

was pledged for a fortnight. Very truly yours, Henry
Irving.

I wrote to Miss Herbert.[61]

To which Ellis countered:

> I hardly know how to reply to your assertion – you
> surely know etc., how could I possibly know anything of
> your private affairs. I am directed to acquaint you that
> the St James's Theatre opens positively on 12th inst,
> and that your attendance is absolutely necessary here at
> the rehearsals that will take place every day next week
> preparatory to the opening.

Irving managed to get his own way with the postponement
of the theatre's opening but his breach of faith was not forgotten by the stage manager. Ellis was not a man to be trifled
with; he had had plenty of experience of different manage-
ments in various theatres and was known for his unique work
of prompt-book transcriptions of Macready's performances.
After his return Irving was given minor parts and the position of acting manager, and the salary that accompanied it,
was transferred elsewhere. This was less of a catastrophe to
Miss Herbert as she too had decided to leave the stage,
though she was prepared to take on a role from time to
time if it appealed to her. Just such a part came her way in
February before retiring, a role which she must have relished.
When they were unable to find a suitable Madame de Pompadour in a translation of the French *Narcisse*, Miss Herbert
had obligingly come forward and offered her services to the
management of the Lyceum Theatre. She was congratulated
for 'giving up the principal in her own theatre in order
to assist the management; it shows a warmth of heart and

generosity seldom to be found.' It must have been a triumphant occasion for our heroine. For one thing the theatre was densely crowded with a distinguished audience of the sort that only graced a special occasion. *The Era* (2 February 1868) commented on Miss Herbert having given the 'fullest effect to the Marchioness de Pompadour, thoroughly realising the eternal graces of the fascinating favourite', and in the final act she played 'with all that delicacy of style and impassioned feeling so characteristic of this popular actress'. Soon to lose a favourite, the audience filling every portion of the theatre was no doubt made up of many of her past adorers.

On 25 April, under the patronage of the Prince of Wales and the Duke of Edinburgh, Madame Celeste took her farewell engagement at the St James's. This was followed by *A Happy Pair* in which two players only, Miss Herbert and William Farren, took part. It was well received and the actress was said to have been 'indeed perfect'. She took her final Benefit on 27 April 1868, appearing as Lady Teazle in her farewell performance. The following year, when Mrs John Wood took over the management of the theatre, Miss Herbert appeared once or twice in some of her old parts. Her last performance was the conclusion of what had been her professional life since her first steps on the Lyceum stage in 1847. Her management was over: there had been successes but, as with her predecessors, it had not been financially profitable.

Two incidents remain predominant in Miss Herbert's career without which she would scarcely be remembered. The one, when as a young woman she attracted the genius of Rossetti's brush and pencil, so that her beauty became an attraction and increased her drawing power to the theatre in which she was acting. Then there was Henry Irving. Though

Boucicault had ensured him the opportunity, it was Miss Herbert who had had the vision to recognise his potential and provide him with a stage. From these beginnings emerged a man who would become the nation's greatest actor, to share the laurels with Garrick and Edmund Kean. 'Surely this justifies her contribution to the English stage.'[62]

9

Abroad and at Home

Louisa was approaching her forties, no longer the slender vision that had so beguiled Rossetti ten years earlier. W. B. Scott, writing to Alice Boyd of a dinner party given by the architect George Edmund Street, described her on 29 May 1874 as 'Mrs Crabb (Miss Herbert) with a voluminous surrounding of blue silk, and a display of bosom'.[63] Tall, with a commanding presence, a fine neck and arms, attributes much favoured by the Victorians, handsome and confident, this intimidating figure was now seeking a domestic life. Marriage was beckoning. Rochfort whom she loved had given her a son, a house, financial support and now she wanted his name and respectability.

In January 1868 Louisa petitioned for divorce on the grounds of Crabb's desertion in 1857. Her sister Emma came from Bristol and testified against Crabb. The whole sordid account was published in *The Era*. Judgment was given in March. Louisa was entitled to a judicial separation on the grounds of adultery but this she had not applied for and a petition for a dissolution of marriage was dismissed. Having failed to get a divorce she went with Rochey to Switzerland that summer of 1868 and on their return to Sidmouth Lodge they announced to the children that they had been married abroad. There were no questions asked, not publicly at least, but Louisa was rarely called anything but Mrs Crabbe until after Rochfort's death, for there had been no divorce and consequently no remarriage.

Rochfort had now come to live at Sidmouth Lodge. His mother having died, the house at Eaton Place was his; his sister and her daughter still lived there though its upkeep was his to maintain. In this new life of semi-respectability the children had no need to refer to their mother as as an actress. Arthur Crabbe went to Eton in April 1871, just after his fourteenth birthday, his 'Parents' address' being given as J. D. Rochfort, 40 Eaton Place (by then of course a stepfather, more or less). Cecil Bayley on the other hand, being an illegitimate child, did not qualify for the same sort of education as Arthur.[64] He was entered at Rugby in 1873 and inscribed as the son of 'John Edward Bayley' of Bolton Gardens, Rochey's and Crabbe's Christian names appearing in tandem.

The 1871 census for Sidmouth Lodge, The Boltons, gives Mrs Edward Crabbe as married with no occupation, Arthur as a scholar. Neither Rochfort nor Cecil Bayley are listed but the ten-year-old Midge is inscribed as Augusta, niece to Louisa and born in Paris. The rigidity of Victorian conventions so cruelly applied to her daughter illumines the harshness of the woman's character in her desire to obliterate all signs of misconduct. There were three domestic servants as well as a governess from Lyon and, besides, a gardener and his wife and two daughters, one an apprentice dressmaker.

Miss Herbert had no regrets in leaving the theatre; she always maintained that she had never cared for acting and had never been able to remember lines. She had her idiosyncrasies too: she put an apple pie by her bed at night as she could not sleep; she rose early and washed her face in the morning dew; and in later life would not dine unless she had on pink stockings.

Old John Maynard died in 1871 at 12 Waterloo Place, Bristol. Astonishingly, this turns out to have been an 'eating house' belonging to a Joseph Wookey, perhaps a friend of the Pottows; he had rooms as well. He left Louisa all he had, £200. In age she resembled him more and more. At Sidmouth Lodge he would always find his mahogany high and upright armchair which Frederick Milbank had had made for him and in which it eased his arthritis to sit. On one such occasion Milbank had a seizure and Emma Pottow, also present, loosened his collar – for which he gratefully recompensed her with a pair of handsome vases. Together with the chair they have been handed down to younger generations.

Now Louisa was retired from the stage a life of travel presented itself in Rochfort's acquisition in 1869 of the schooner *Leda*. Built at Cowes in 1849 she had had two or three owners and had been entered in the Royal Yacht Club in 1851. She weighed 132 tons, her length was 88.9 ft, beam 18.7 ft. Cowes was her port of registration, Rochfort the owner and Eaton Place the address. From 1869 until 1880 a family migration took place every year in August to the end of October. A crew for that size yacht would have probably consisted of a captain (at £2.10s a week), a mate (£1.10s), boatswain (£1.6s), five able seamen (25s a week each), a steward (£1.10s), assistant steward (16s), cook (£1.10s) and assistant cook (16s).[65] In the early days their movements were cautious. The first summer of 1869 saw them at Ushant, Dartmouth and Boulogne, but before long the delights of Leghorn, Elba, Belle Isle, Dieppe and Trouville took them further. In July 1873 they witnessed the Shah of Persia's review at sea from Ryde; from Naples in the same year

Arthur and Cecil remembered having been sent back to school in September, a journey undertaken by rail and diligence. A sojourn at Bordeaux enabled Rochfort and Louisa to pay a call at Lord Ernest Bruce's house in Biarritz, the Villa Marbella, although the owner was absent. But this was a very old and probably intimate friendship dating far back to Louisa's youth. He was one of the very few people who wrote to her and called her by her Christian name.

Rossetti and Miss Herbert met rarely; his wife had died in 1862 and he had moved from their old rooms to a handsome house in Cheyne Walk overlooking the river. It was initially too large for him on his own, so his brother William Michael Rossetti, George Meredith and Swinburne joined him there. Rossetti was painting an oil head of Miss Herbert in about 1864 from an earlier drawing and it may have been when she had come to sit for him that she was shown in and sat down beside a table covered with a heavy chenille cloth. Her waiting was interrupted by a pinch on her ankle and from under the fringe emerged Algernon Swinburne on all fours.

On 30 December 1871 Rossetti was invited to dinner on 8 January 1872. 'I know you seldom go out,' Louisa wrote, 'but I look forward so much to the pleasure of seeing you once more that I trust you will make an exception to your rule – in my favour.' The writing paper was narrowly bordered in black for her father and she signed herself 'Louisa Crabbe'. He must have replied immediately as she wrote again the next day that they would dine at half past seven o'clock which she hoped would not be inconvenient to him. Rochey was collecting all the portrait studies of her that he could find and perhaps they hoped that over dinner Rossetti might give them information of their whereabouts.

Frederick Sandys was engaged on a painting of Miss

Herbert as Cleopatra in 1873 (untraced); this she gave to Mrs Frederick Milbank on the latter's birthday in 1876. If the portrayal on canvas was to represent the 'serpent of old Nile' (could this have been the intimation of the gift?), the image that Rochfort made from it in 1877 on a creamware pottery dish[66] depicts a woman reclining three-quarter length on a tiger skin and from the small basket held on her lap she raises the deadly asp to her lips. Her red gold hair is bound with a velvet ribbon and fastened by a diamond ornament. There is no means of knowing whether this white-skinned Victorian Cleopatra daringly clad in classical dress is a true reproduction of Sandys's work.

Portraiture, one might say, took hold in the Crabbe family in the 1870s. Joseph Middleton Jopling's watercolour portrait of Midge was hung at the Royal Academy Summer Exhibition of 1874, although probably painted a year or two earlier. Millais, a friend of the artist, was always said by the sitter to have had a hand in the work. Louise Jopling had made chalk likenesses of Midge as *Alsace* and *Lorraine* in 1875 and finding her pictures badly placed at the Royal Academy she had written off to the Secretary and 'priced my pictures at 60gns each'. 'M[ilbank]', looking at *Alsace* said 'he was flabbergasted at the price – he thought it would have been £150, and that it was well worth £200.'[67] Mrs Jopling, while a good deal younger than Miss Herbert, and whose life was not without irregularities, had an eye to the main chance (in which she and Louisa were alike) and was something of an ally. In March 1876 she wrote of 'trotting off to the Rothschilds', in spite of Rochfort 'calling at the eleventh hour to ask me to go to the Boat-race with him and the Crabbes'.[68] She felt tempted as the morning was so lovely – 'but it was just as well that I was engaged, I thought.' Perhaps no woman

[85]

Midge, *by J. M. Jopling, c. 1873*

alone cared to be seen around with a couple of tarnished reputation. However, later in the same month she recorded in a letter written at midnight on her return from Sidmouth Lodge, that Miss Herbert had called on her that morning to say she was acting at the Consumption Hospital (Brompton) and would Mrs Jopling like to come and then go back to supper. She had enjoyed herself enormously (unfortunately not mentioning the names of the other guests); 'I had a motto improvised for me. Everybody was amusing themselves by making them on those present.'[69]

That same year Miss Herbert had acted in *Up the Ladder* at Limerick, and in 1883, a real veteran now, she was well received as the Baroness Ocker in the English version of Sardou's *Fedora*, given at the Haymarket, Squire Bancroft and Marie Wilton heading the cast.

An unwelcome arrival in London was that of Ada, a niece from Australia, who wanted to be an actress. Her masterful aunt said she had no talent whatsoever and the quicker she was packed off home the better, as she drank like a fish. She would lie face downwards on her trunk doing swimming strokes to keep her figure but had cold water thrown at her when her actions suggested insobriety.

Rochfort continued to paint on china and used his talent to good effect in the chapel of the Hospital for Consumption and Diseases of the Chest, Fulham Road (later known as the Brompton Hospital), where he was a Governor and served on the Committee of Management from 1867 to 1879, becoming Vice-Chairman in the latter part of this period. Besides other sub-committees he was active on the Building Committee of the South Block between 1872 and 1882.[70] The chapel, built by E. B. Lamb in 1850, surrounded on three sides by fields, was received as a work of importance by

The Builder; the *Ecclesiologist* on the other hand reported that 'those who can swallow this chapel . . . can swallow anything.'[71] Rochfort decorated the small stone font in 1875 with painted panels depicting scenes from the New Testament in blue on a gold ground, dating them and signing them with his initials.[72] Shortly before his retirement from the Hospital committee he painted fifteen tiles, each with the arms of a committee member, including those of Queen Victoria and the Prince of Wales.[73]

10

Departures

Odd, but probably welcomed by those at Sidmouth Lodge, was the move of the Milbank family from Cromwell Place to 2 Moreton Gardens. This was a very large house indeed, newly-built, stucco-faced, forming the angle of the Old Brompton Road and the northern point of The Boltons. Milbank had a stained-glass window introduced facing the Old Brompton Road made by the William Morris firm, depicting angels with cymbals and musical instruments. Jenny Lind, the singer, had a much smaller house (1 Moreton Gardens) which lay between Sidmouth Lodge and the Milbanks', but from the back window of No. 2 one could look straight into Miss Herbert's garden. There was, presumably, a perfectly sophisticated relationship between Milbank, his one-time mistress, and Rochfort. Midge was by then sixteen and probably not yet aware of her parentage. Louisa hoped for an early marriage for her daughter; she would have liked her off her hands and no questions asked. Illegitimate, and an actress's daughter, for all her astonishing beauty there was no likelihood of a dazzling marriage.

In the autumn of 1876 Louisa paid a long visit to Castle Fraser in Aberdeenshire and again in 1877, taking Midge with her. It is probable that Colonel Frederick Mackenzie Fraser was also a friend of Rochfort. His first wife had died in

1874 and he did not remarry until 1879, but from a subsequent report it seems quite likely that on Louisa's side at least there was the hope of a marriage for her daughter. Aberdeenshire offered a remote and incurious neighbour-hood, but the scheme failed.

Now over fifty, Rochey was beginning to find travels on *Leda* fatiguing. He and Louisa favoured a more tranquil mode of life and a warmer winter haven. *Leda* was sold in 1880 and the Villa Pleasance in Monte Carlo acquired, to be exchanged two years later for the Villa Philippe, just outside the town, where they spent the winter and spring, including regular visits to Paris. With the purchase of the villa in the South of France, Sidmouth Lodge was to let and Miss Herbert, replying to Mr Schott (husband of Fanny Cornforth, Rossetti's housekeeper, mistress and model) who was prob-ably making inquiries on Rossetti's behalf, begged to inform him 'that her house is to be let *furnished* for the *winter*'.[74] To Mrs William Morris Rossetti wrote: 'I have asked Watts to take a look at the Boltons but think there must be some fag-end or lease or other inconvenience about it such as rental. It is the house where Miss Herbert (Mrs Crabb) lived for so many years, and I had no idea she had left it. Perhaps she is dead.'[75] (She lived another forty odd years.)

After the disposal of the schooner they remained mostly in England for the summers, at St Leonards, the Pavilion, Folkestone, at Ascot, at Oatlands Park Hotel, while in Lon-don the garden at Sidmouth Lodge offered the delight of shady trees and quiet. Beatrix Potter was a neighbour living over the road at 2 Bolton Gardens – she mentions a pair 'of starlings from Mrs Crabb's garden'.[76] Augusts were spent at Bad Homburg or Baden Baden.

The year 1881 had started badly, for Arthur, the most

cherished of Louisa's children, had sailed for the Transvaal in January with his regiment, the 3rd King's Own Hussars. However, barely five months later he had returned having seen no fighting, as new peace negotiations between the British Government and the Transvaal had been recognised.

At Bad Homburg that summer Rochey and Louisa were joined by a very old friend, Lord Ernest Bruce, now the 3rd Marquess of Ailesbury. His diaries[77] for August and September 1881 record many meetings: 'Dined at table d'hôte, Hotel de Russia. Met Mother Crabbe and Midge at dinner.' (It is questionable whether the fair Louisa would have appreciated such a designation.) 'Gave Mother Crabbe and Midge and Rochfort a dinner in my rooms where I was very credibly done justice.' 'Went in the evening to Mother Crabbe and had a cup of chocolate and heard Midge sing and play to me very prettily some hymns.' This is a sad picture of Midge, dragged about by her mother in the company of her mother's lover – could anything be less respectable? It is probable that Louisa passed as 'Mrs Rochfort' when they travelled but it is certain that all those who had known her from the past, or knew of her, referred to her as 'Mrs Crabbe'. Arthur Sullivan was also at Bad Homburg that August and played tennis with Midge and 'in the evening Mrs and Miss Crabbe and Rochfort' had dined with him in his rooms. There was more tennis, afternoon walks with Midge and finally 'Heard Miss Crabbe sing.'

Presumably Sullivan had been known to Miss Herbert in earlier days; possibly through her involvement with W. S. Gilbert at the St James's Theatre. He was a friend of Edward Crabb who, after vanishing twenty-five years ago from this story, now reappears as a man of substance with many acquaintances. In the 1880s he is known to have had rooms

Arthur Bingham Crabbe

in Granville House, Granville Place, close to Portman Square. Dining with Millais in Palace Gate in the summer of 1881 in the company of Trollope, Hardy and others, he won six pounds from Trollope at whist, the novelist's favourite card game. There were more dinners in the following years when Crabb was the host and entertained Sullivan and other friends. Crabb rented Glenham House in 1887, the property of the Duke of Hamilton in Great Glenham, Suffolk.[78] This was a big house in a park of seventy acres where he held large shooting parties. In 1891 he left Great Glenham and took a short lease of Benacre Hall, also in Suffolk. His travelling companions abroad – to Paris, Algiers, Verona – often included Sullivan. He finally went to live near Dorking, Surrey, at Bentsbrock House, of a substantial size in a three-acre garden, and died there at Christmas-time in 1904, leaving most of his estate, which included town plots in Lethbridge, West Canada, and shares in mining, to a nephew.

Rochfort's health was failing and a slow deterioration set in. In the spring of 1885, on their way home from Monte Carlo, he died in Paris on 24 May at the Hotel Liverpool, rue de Castiglione, at the age of fifty-eight from a degenerative condition. He was buried at Brompton Cemetery in the Rochfort grave. There is no record of the intensity of Louisa's grief though it must have been severe. At his death he left something between one and a half to two million pounds in today's money. In his will, completed in 1884, he described himself as of 40 Eaton Place and Villa Philippe. This last, together with Sidmouth Lodge, he bequeathed to 'My dearly beloved wife Louisa Ruth Rochfort otherwise Crabbe and I make this devise to confirm her in the possession of such properties in case it should appear that she is not legally and equitably entitled thereto.' A carefully worded document to circumvent any questions regarding her married state.

A diamond necklace, the residue of his estate, and general belongings were for Louisa, as well as 40 Eaton Place after his sister's death and the removal of his niece elsewhere. Arthur Crabbe was generously remembered, Cecil Bayley, his own son, less so; £3,000 was his inheritance as he had already received certain sums of money. Finally, an *objet de vertu* was left to Sir Frederick Milbank. The watercolour of *Writing on the Sand* by Rossetti, which the artist had made 'for Miss Herbert (rightly Mrs Crabbe)',[79] was sold at Christie's just a year after Rochey's death.

Lord Ailesbury's visits to The Boltons increased. During the summer of Rochfort's death which Louisa spent at Sidmouth Lodge, his diary[80] reveals that even in the previous year Midge was perhaps the greater attraction. He was assiduous in his invitations. Expeditions to Hurlingham which included Midge and 'capital dinner'; dinner at Mother Crabbe's 'to eat a bit of my own venison; Midge looking very pretty. Spent some of the time in the garden with her.' On one occasion he had a walk with her and 'passed one of the pleasantest afternoons perhaps of my life'. Even 'Froggy'[81] (otherwise Arthur Crabbe) made an appearance and dined Lord Ailesbury at Hounslow where he was with his regiment; they had 'a capital dinner'. And at the end of August he gave 'dear little Midge and Cecil with Mother Crabbe a capital dinner, wine etc and very cheap'. He was now seventy-six and would die the next year; Midge was twenty-four with no husband and was aware that Louisa aspired to an arranged marriage for her rather than one of the heart. Indeed recently, sick with apprehension, she had overheard her mother interview a drunken Irish peer in the room next door.

Cecil Bayley, 1879

Since Rochfort's death Louisa had called herself by his name; no one would dispute it with a grieving widow and it gave a certain air of propriety as she made preparations to leave Sidmouth Lodge and live elsewhere. Belgrave Mansions, two large town houses built at the bottom of Grosvenor Gardens on a triangular piece of ground, had been turned into handsome apartments. The houses designed by Cundy III in the mid-1860s were in Second Empire style, lofty and 'of an elaborateness and colourfulness unknown in London'.[82] Here she was close to Mrs Hildyard, still at Eaton Place. She retained the Villa Philippe at Monte Carlo for another two years (where Clement Scott noted that he found her looking as well and as young as ever) and Midge was always with her. Louisa's introduction to Albert Edward Prince of Wales, when as an actress she had been admired by him at the Olympic and St James's Theatres, ensured a degree of sympathy for the ravishing Midge. At a ball at Sandringham when wearing a dress eccentrically designed by her mother of flesh pink, unadorned and relieved only by black cocks' feathers surrounding the décolletage like a necklace, Midge had earned the equivocal name of the Undressed Crabbe. A flirtation with the Prince ensued, short notes from him have survived. When Midge was at Monte Carlo in 1886 and the Prince at Cannes a meeting was arranged by him, the Prince writing:

Just 2 lines to say that I hope to come to M Carlo tomorrow for a few hours but quite incog: so please do not mention it – If you will be on the terrace between 1 & 1.30 I shall hope to see you then. *Yrs* very sincerely

AE

His kindness to her was in evidence when in the following

year Captain Conyers Surtees of the Coldstream Guards saw her one Sunday morning in the English Church at Nice and determined against his father's unrelenting fury to marry this young woman of irregular background and with no money. The Prince had spoken to the prospective father-in-law in Midge's favour – which perhaps made it worse – but to no effect. A captain's pay was little enough on which to marry, so together the young couple confronted Sir Frederick Milbank, now an elderly roué as depicted by 'Ape' in *Vanity Fair* (1875). This was his third settlement on Midge, once soon after her birth, again in 1873 when she was twelve, and now at the time of her marriage which was arranged for 27 June 1887 at St Peter's, Eaton Square, though it had all but foundered when Midge was seen to bite her bread at lunch instead of breaking it.[83] On her wedding morning the Prince of Wales wrote to her from Marlborough House:

> You will I hope accept the accompanying bouquet – from me as a souvenir of today. With my very *best* wishes for your happiness now. Yours very sincerely
>
> ALBERT EDWARD

Midge walked up the aisle holding two bouquets, that of the Prince and the one given her by the bridegroom; her mother and a member of the Milbank family were witnesses and Arthur Crabbe gave her away.

Two years later when living in Constantinople Midge was in Athens with her husband, then military attaché, in order to attend the wedding of the Duke of Sparta to Sophia, daughter of the widowed Empress Frederick of Prussia and thus niece of the Prince of Wales whose Royal Yacht *Osborne* had arrived, commanded by Captain the Hon. Hedworth Lambton (later to change his name to Meux).[84] A

Midge, *by S. M. Fisher, 1889*

contemporary diarist and friend of Midge wrote that the Prince 'likes talking to [her] better than anyone, he is awfully fond of her, but quite friendly, he doesn't flirt with her one bit.'[85] Captain Lambton however was known to be a scandalous flirt and made a deep impression on Midge and they remained close friends.[86]

Of Louisa's sons, the younger, Cecil Bayley, read Roman Law at Heidelberg University and later went to Rhodesia as Secretary at the Law Department. He suffered from bad health and served at home during the First World War.

Arthur Bingham Crabbe, who fell off a penny-farthing bicycle killing a hen and breaking an ankle so that for the rest of a long life he wore a wooden or metal foot, was a reckless character in other respects. Spoilt in youth and doted on by his mother, he was involved in a few unsavoury escapades. His first cousin, a solicitor on the Pottow side, was allotted the task of fixing a separation between Arthur and a girl he had made pregnant while at The Curragh. She had begged for marriage, to which he had agreed, but later they decided to separate. He would pay her £2 a week, provide her with a sum of money for clothes and ship her off to New York. However, Arthur was now employing a detective as he had grounds for belief that though the girl had professed to have had his child it belonged in fact to her sister. Arthur hoped for grounds for divorce. This incident followed close upon one to do with a girl called 'Jessie' and was soon followed by an action for breach of promise, 'Duncan v. Crabbe'. The *Daily Mail* reported it as 'no ordinary case'. Miss Mabel Duncan was one of the 'alluring mousmee who carry tea in dainty attitudes and play on sweet samisen' in *The Geisha* at Daly's Theatre, and Crabbe was 'no less a person than a brave gentleman who holds Her Majesty's commission'. The case was adjourned by consent. Arthur served in the Boer War and eventually married but this ended in disaster. Always short of money he died at Montreux in 1945.

While living in London Louisa had attended St Peter's Church, Cranley Gardens, and had sat under the Revd Francis Byng (son of the 3rd Earl of Stafford). On moving to Hove in the 1890s, however, she converted to the Church of Rome and with absolution of her confessed sins settled down to a life of invincible rectitude. The Hove Directories listed her as Madame Rochfort, living at No. 3 Grand Avenue Mansions, a depressingly dark flat facing the sea (and still standing), with large cavernous rooms and Rossetti's drawings on the walls. She led a dignified life, dressed to the nines, even when severe arthritis later made a bath chair a necessity. Her old friend Charles Mathews, once familiar on Hove lawns, was dead but Henry Irving, staying at the Norfolk Hotel, Brighton, would visit her and rehearse some of his longer speeches.[87] When Louisa was in London she would lodge at the celebrated Langham Hotel, Portland Place, built in Italianate style in the 1860s, 'a leviathan of its kind'. For the visitor it was said to unite the comforts of a club with those of a private home.

A year before his death Rochfort had given her a book for her birthday very much to her taste: *The Practical Housewife*, inscribed from 'her affectionate husband'. Domesticity was her chief interest now and in 1894 she published *The St James's Cookery Book* which included helpful hints on 'invalid food' and a lengthy Advice to Bread-Makers.

With the years came a loss of memory. A great-niece remembered an alarming visit to 'Madame Rochfort' when her great-aunt removed a boiled sweet from a jar, put it in her mouth, sucked it for a moment or two, replaced it in the jar and offered it to the child. If thwarted in the least degree she would shriek the house down and as her temper deteriorated her homicidal tendencies became more pronounced. But her vitality was still extraordinary. She pinched and banged people about and accused them of all sorts of sins of omission and commission. Slipping off her chair onto the floor she was quick to accuse her old maid of having knocked her down.

She died on 10 April 1921 at the age of ninety with Midge beside her, having been unconscious for some days, and was buried in Brompton Cemetery with Rochfort – to the anger of his remaining family: a Roman Catholic adulteress was not welcome in the tomb of Irish Protestants.

The Brewer's Wife

Beer, beer, glorious beer!
Fill yerself right up to 'ere – 'ere – 'ere;
Up with the sale of it,
Down with a pail of it,
Glorious, glor – r – r – ious beer!

I

The Meux Brewery

Henry Bruce Meux at the age of twenty-two in the year 1878 was, one could say, seduced by a pair of violet eyes.

In the early 1880s, when Whistler was painting his two whole-length portraits of Valerie Suzie Meux, the uninformed might rightly have considered that the sitter, the wife of a wealthy man (soon to become a baronet), had secured for herself a most enviable position in life's worldly late-Victorian campaign. To see her bejewelled and cloaked in self-confidence and white furs in the one portrait and in the other glancing out alluringly beneath her becoming round straw hat, as bewitching a pose as might have enthralled any of her lovers and had indeed captured her youthful adorer, is to mark her as a woman of determination, stepping with fierce ambition from prostitution to a life of wealth. Here, though, was the stumbling block which halted her advance into the world she craved: her husband's family on his maternal side would not accept her, neither would Society.

Of her own family there appears to have been none. The daughter of a mother unknown and probably unmarried, cared for by an anonymous foster mother, carrying the name of Langdon of a supposed father but whether authentic or a fabrication was never revealed. She spoke fleetingly of a career on the stage in more youthful years but this was interpreted as a turn or two in pantomime, possibly in London's old Surrey Music Hall, in transformation scenes, perhaps as Columbine.

Young Harry Meux was the only child of an immensely rich father, Sir Henry Meux, 2nd Baronet, of Meux Brewery. The family of Meux, originally from Meaux in France, pronouncing their name 'Mews' while the Brewery sounded the final 'x', had a long history holding land in Wiltshire dating from the seventeenth century. A baronetcy had been acquired in the eighteenth century but was extinguished owing to a poverty of male heirs, though it flourished again later.

One Thomas Meux, merchant, had married Elizabeth, sister of Sir William Massingberd, Bt, of Gunby Hall, Lincolnshire, who dying without issue in 1723 had left Gunby Hall to his widowed sister for her life and subsequently to her eldest son, William, who now, according to the wish of the testator, assumed the name of his benefactor. Her second son went into the Church, as had others of the family, and it was this man's son, Richard, who embarked on the beer trade.

Richard's wife, Mary Brougham, was the aunt of Henry Brougham, a happy if fortuitous occurrence. In 1830 Lord Brougham, as he had become, used his influence to secure a baronetcy for his first cousin, Henry Meux, son of Richard and Mary. Although possibly contrived for the proud recipient, it was a fair acknowledgement of Henry's very successful progression as a brewer. He had advanced so well in his trade, had worked with such enthusiasm and energy that he had acquired the Horseshoe Brewery in the first quarter of the nineteenth century, premises which fronted on to the Tottenham Court Road on the present site of the

Dominion Theatre and stretched along the side of what is now New Oxford Street. Stout iron gates guarded the entrance while adjoining, and easily approached by the public, stood the Horseshoe Tavern, the Brewery's 'tap' where the Meux commodity was always available. This was also a haunt of street women looking for a companion for the night and shelter or at least a jug of beer or porter. Its situation, adjacent to one of the seamiest quarter of London, ensured a disreputable clientele of prostitutes, pimps and their acolytes.

The Brewery was soon renamed Meux and remained at No. 268 Tottenham Court Road until 1921 when it moved to Nine Elms, Battersea, where it stayed until the company closed down in 1961. The tavern retained its original name and its original custom.

Sir Henry Meux, wanting a house close to his business, acquired No. 19 Great Russell Street, to which he took his wife and family. However, as he grew rich, desire for a more impressive address and a country seat in keeping with his status led him in 1820 to an estate in Hertfordshire, Theobalds Park, Waltham Cross, of which he bought the lease. When he died in 1841, his son, another Henry, the 2nd Baronet, came into a fortune of something close to a quarter of a million pounds at the age of twenty-four. His sisters, and there were three of them, each received a handsome legacy.

This son was a direct reverse of his father, He understood rather too well the pleasures and obligations of a rich man. His immense talents for enjoyment were harnessed to a reckless extravagance. Hunting and game shooting were perhaps predominant and here his French chef could vouch for just over 2,000 guests for shooting parties in one month. Deer stalking required an estate in the Highlands if only as a duty

Menx's Brewery, Tottenham Court Road, 1830

to his friends and his remodelling and enlarging of Theobalds reflected his appetite for hospitality. To accommodate his many guests, a billiard room and a conservatory were added and space allowed for balls and entertaining on a grand scale. More land was purchased to extend the property. His London house, 41 Upper Brook Street, where he lived from 1845 to 1857, dated from 1736. In 1851 the conditions of a new lease imposed certain improvements in accordance with drawings of Thomas Cundy the younger, adding pilasters on the upper floors and arched ground floor windows.[88]

And where in this delightful litany of young Sir Henry's extravagance was the management or concern for the Brewery apparent? The answer is they were non-existent. Money flowed from the Brewery without his assistance and he was content to leave it at that, having placed the management into the capable hands of his brother-in-law, William St Julian Arabin. Mr Sergeant Arabin, the husband of Henry's elder sister Mary, was a noted member of the Bar and held a judiciary appointment at the Old Bailey. He was a shrewd man of affairs and his assiduity was repaid with the sum of £1,500 a year.

2

Enter the Ailesburys

In this life of pleasure and conviviality Henry Meux had probably met his future wife, Louisa Brudenell-Bruce, during a London season. She was already twenty when she married him (old for the times), possibly pointing to a dearth of suitors or perhaps such as there were had been considered unsuitable by her father, Lord Ernest Brudenell-Bruce, of 6 St George's Place, Hyde Park Corner, second son of the 1st Marquess of Ailesbury, Vice Chamberlain to the Household and Member of Parliament for Marlborough (and not unknown in the earlier pages of this book). The likelihood of an insignificant marriage portion may have hampered a fit connection.

When in 1878 Lord Ernest, at sixty-seven, succeeded a relentlessly extravagant father and elder brother to become 3rd Marquess, he also inherited a large estate at a time when landed property was suffering diminishing returns owing to agricultural depression. Savernake Forest alone, held by the family for 800 years, had an extent of sixteen miles of wood fencing to keep in repair. The palatial house, Tottenham Park, rebuilt on Burlington's earlier structure by Cundy in 1820, on which great sums had been expended to furnish and to acquire pictures needed a bottomless purse to maintain.[89]

However, in the years 1846 and 1847 the 1st Marquess

had made two lucrative deals with the railways for main lines to run through his land. From the London South West Direct Railway the contract was for £30,000 though this was never built. The Great Western agreed to pay £14,000 for seventy acres of land and £5,000 for 'residential damages' to Tottenham Park which lay within a mile of the line. From this, Lord Ailesbury obtained the special treatment (often accorded to aristocrats) of a station at Great Bedwyn and the halt of 'Two first class up trains and two first class down trains . . . at such times as the Marquess of Ailesbury or his heirs shall select from each fresh timetable'.[90]

A further strain on the estate and a cause for paucity of money when Lord Ernest came to inherit was the unassailable fact that two dowager marchionesses, his stepmother and his elder brother's widow, and that brother's daughter-in-law (widow of the eldest son) had claims on handsome jointures from the estate. His stepmother, born Maria Tollemache, had been a leading figure in Society and in old age 'the evergreen marchioness was a constant frequenter of London parties and country race courses and was to be seen in Hyde Park with flaxen hair (or wig) driving two ponies, generally preceded by two outriders.'[91] She lived on until 1893. After Lord Ernest's death there would still be his own widow to join the other dowagers, all three ladies living into the 1890s. (His daughter-in-law married again.)

With seven children to provide for, Lord Ernest may have seen it as some compensation that when his daughter Louisa married into trade she had at least attracted an exceedingly rich man. Most probably her alliance with a brewery did not find favour with her family though it is more than likely that she was determined on a rich match which would enable her to escape the rows at home, chiefly occasioned by the delinquencies of her siblings – she was the eldest in a batch of five brothers and two sisters. Possibly her own erratic behaviour in the years ahead had its roots in a harsh upbringing. While her letters show a great deal of self-pity there is scant affection for either parent.

Her grandfather, the 1st Marquess, died in the early days of January 1856, to be succeeded by her uncle, who, though married for close on twenty years, had no children, the heir presumptive to the marquessate being her father, Lord Ernest. A family death and funeral of some consequence in the mid-nineteenth century would have entailed many months of mourning. Unwilling to lead a life of further restriction, Louisa was married in Paris by the Revd Thomas Hale, the Embassy chaplain, to Sir Henry Meux on 19 January 1856 at the British Embassy, probably in what was then the smaller dining-room, used as a chapel, behind the state dining-room. Both parents of the bride were present and signed the register, as well as Lord Cowley, the British Ambassador, and his wife. Louisa's seventeen-year-old brother George, as heir apparent to his father, also attended. (He died from a weak constitution at Ajaccio while still in his twenties, achieving little but a reputation for dissipation.) The witness on Sir Henry's side was his paternal aunt Marianne, wife of Sir William Bowyer-Smijth, 11th Baronet and Member of Parliament for South Essex, lending a pleasing image of respectability to the bridegroom's side of the proceedings.

Of this marriage there was one child only, Henry Bruce, or young Harry, born on 21 November 1856 at his father's London house in Upper Brook Street. Within three years of Harry's birth his father showed grave signs of lunacy. Total silence envelops the source or the symptoms. It seems possible that syphilis may have been its cause, common enough at that time and certainly Sir Henry could have been a candidate for infection.

The estate in the Highlands, Glen Morriston, Inverness-shire, had been purchased in 1856; a year later the Meux family moved to a house in Belgrave Square. A portrait of Louisa by Richard Buckner hung in the Royal Academy Summer Exhibition of 1859. By now her own uncertain temperament was proving a difficulty in the upbringing of her son; she also admitted to the impossibility of undertaking the running of a household in which Sir Henry was a patient of unsound mind. This duty was therefore transferred to his sister, Mary Arabin, who lived with him and her husband in Belgrave Square, moving to 30 Grosvenor Street in 1868. She was still in charge of her brother in 1870, settling at 36 Grosvenor Square with a 'salary' of £10,500. Louisa went to live in France, chiefly in Paris, on an income of £15,000, moving from house to hotel from the South of France to Switzerland, never seeing her son or returning to England and always steadfastly complaining of her lot and of real or imagined slights.

3

Our Hero, Young Harry

With Sir Henry's mental collapse arose the responsibilities of his estate. These the Court of Chancery committeed to Lord Ernest and to Mr Dudley Coutts Marjoribanks, Liberal Member for Berwick-on-Tweed, who already had a small share in the Brewery partnership. A capable if self-seeking man of business and an *éminence grise* in the financial affairs of the Brewery, he was shortly to be given a baronetcy and raised to the peerage as the 1st Baron Tweedmouth in 1881.

Young Harry Meux, who on his mother's side was of aristocratic if impoverished descent, was set to inherit on his coming of age the greater part of his father's vast fortune, the bulk of which constituted the invested Brewery profits. At nine years old he was made a ward of court with a grant of £2,200 a year, Lord Ernest and Marjoribanks standing as guardians. In 1870 he went to Eton and rowed in the Eton VIII in 1875.[92] Unlike his father who was up at Christ Church, Oxford, Harry entered Trinity College, Cambridge in 1875 where (or so his guardians conjectured) he was less likely to follow in his father's dissipated footsteps. There he joined the Third Trinity, a boat club for Eton and Westminster men, but left at the end of the Lent term, 1878, and did not graduate.[93] He had more enjoyable things to do.

When Harry came of age in November 1877 Sir Dudley

Marjoribanks proposed that he should join the Meux firm in partnership with himself, thus assuring his own fortunes by obtaining a half share of the partnership profits. With youth and money at his disposal, no parent to launch him into decent society and a grandfather at odds with his own family, it is not surprising that Harry fell into raffish company.[94]

Holborn and its purlieus would not have been home ground for someone living in Upper Brook Street unless he were bent on tasting the distractions on offer in the stews and generally squalid quarters of the metropolis such as this vicinity was known to be. But here it was that Harry encountered his future wife, Val Reece, as she was commonly called. Some irony may be detected in the fact that Sir Dudley Marjoribanks, who considered Harry 'most fastidious in his tastes', may have introduced him to this unsavoury district by taking him to the Brewery's headquarters in Tottenham Court Road on office business and introducing him as the new family partner. With its questionable reputation the Horseshoe Tavern adjoining the Brewery was a jolly port of call for Harry and, so report goes, for Val too – if in another sense. Whether it was there, in this easy-come, easy-go environment, or whether at the Casino de Venise in Holborn that they met is uncertain.

In earlier days the Casino Tap, Holborn, entertained an exceptionally low class of company. Tennyson and D. G. Rossetti had walked past the newly named Holborn Casino together in the early hours of 18 September 1855. They had spent the evening with the Brownings in Dorset Street where Tennyson had read aloud his 'Maud' to the assembled company while Rossetti had silently made his now well-known sketch of the poet edifying his audience. Rossetti was on his way home to Chatham Place, Blackfriars Bridge; Tennyson was in lodgings for a few days. They noticed that the cabs outside the Holborn Casino were still busy at 2 a.m.,[95] for this was a resort for 'fast' men and dissolute women where on festive nights the 'rollicking rams' of the period let themselves go.[96] But now, some twenty years later, renamed the Casino de Venise, and more than a cut above the Horseshoe Tavern, though still a haunt of easy women, it offered 'dancing to a celebrated band'. Elegantly fitted up with much more space for jostling couples and the pleasures of a 'bob-hop', it was 'a cheerful, bouncy, sort of place where the easy pick-ups were the great attraction'. Women went well-dressed, but no respectable woman would be seen there.

If not a hostess, Val was certainly an *habituée* of this rather shady dance hall which was appreciated by the 'apprentice-lawyers, young ships' officers, clerks, well-off young tradesmen'[97] who frequented it; but since neither spirits or wine were sold, the friendly old bar at the Horseshoe Tavern may have been the likelier meeting place, given that Val's engagement ring was inscribed:[98]

> To B----y old Val
> From drunken old Hal

Harry was twenty-two when he left Cambridge at Easter 1878. His mother, writing from Paris later that year, referred to his yacht which he had left at Rouen, probably that summer, with 'this woman Val Reece on board' with one of his friends while 'he was gong on in a fine way with those horrid *french* women in Paris' and quite 'running wild with these *low* people'.[99]

Val Reece was a handsome woman of intelligence, rising thirty, aware of her attractions and arresting good looks, with a lively if forward manner not exempt from vulgarity. A corporal in the Life Guards, under whose name she pursued her occupation, was her present lover and her pimp, though his *modus operandi* may have been even more unscrupulous – a report went that Reece 'frequently visits him arrayed in civilian garb and bills for a very large amount have been put into circulation, although where the proceeds have gone is not clear.'[100] Surely suggestive of blackmail.

4

The Scandalous Marriage

Whether through coercion, blackmail or perfect love the marriage took place on 27 October 1878 at All Souls, Langham Place, by common licence, thus enabling the pair to avoid banns being read with all the accompanying publicity. Valerie Susan Langdon, a spinster, 'of full age', gave as her father's name, 'William Langdon (dec.), Gentleman', and her address as All Souls, Langham Place, St Marylebone – as did Harry. The three witnesses are of names unknown. The scurrilous *Truth* hastened to point out that Miss Reece ('no longer *dans la première jeunesse*') had led to the hymeneal altar Mr Meux and 'has landed the largest fish which has floated in the matrimonial waters for some time'.[101] In short it was seen as a marriage that had been contrived by the woman in question.

Lord Ernest (by now the 3rd Marquess), Harry's grandfather and sometime guardian, had been alerted that his grandson had come a matrimonial cropper by a note signed 'Your affectionate granddaughter, Valerie'.[102] The family was stunned. The first to raise her wail of shocked outrage was his mother, Lady Louisa Meux. Writing to her eldest surviving brother, Lord Henry Bruce, from Paris – 15 avenue du Bois de Boulogne – where she had received the news of Harry's marriage to 'the *kept mistress* of Captain [Corporal] Reece', she expressed her sense of disappointment in her father who

Valerie Meux, c. 1880

had every confidence in him and who in all his letters
always speaks of him as the best boy that ever lived and
one who has never given him one moment's trouble. I
believed him to be quiet and a perfect gentleman and I
never therefore for an instant thought it possible he
should be mad enough to *marry* anybody of that *class*,
besides he ought to have married for rank and I regret
that no one in the family got him to marry at least a
lady. Write to me all you know of this disgraceful affair
and tell me if my mother intends to receive her. I hear
she is well known and has been knocking about London
for at least ten years and is five years older than him.[103]

A further agitated letter followed at the end of the month:
despair 'at the terrible affair'; wishing to see Harry but 'for
God's sake dont talk of his coming here abroad with that

dreadful woman'; maddened by the thought that 'the Corporal in the Life Guards is fleecing him like anything'; awful to think 'such a nice boy should now be on the road to ruin. He must get rid of that woman and that infamous set who *rob* him.' She went on to blame her father, 'and you all for not getting him into proper society instead of these *filthy low english*'.

Sir Dudley Marjoribanks, whose guardianship had ceased a year before, was not slow to take into account that Harry's wife had been the predominant mover in the marriage campaign and must be forbidden interference with her husband in the Brewery concerns. But first a letter to Lord Ailesbury:

> We had indeed all great cause for grief and astonishment at the egregious folly of poor Harry, and that *he* of all youngsters should have destroyed himself by marrying such a woman. We considered him most fastidious in his tastes, always giving naturally and unknowingly preference to a refined beauty and manners – so much so that we always knew the kind of girl he would take to and get on with – poor boy.[104]

Some short time was allowed to elapse before Marjoribanks moved into the attack with Lord Henry Bruce, who was now taking over these family matters from his father. The 3rd Marquess was both getting on in years and wilting somewhat under the financial burden of the three dowagers. *Vanity Fair* had published a cartoon of the 3rd Marquess, 'a bowed and rather haggard figure – wearing an expression of profound pessimism', bearing the simple caption: 'Three Dowagers'.[105]

With Harry's first step to enhance what he hoped might be Valerie's entrance into Society by buying her £10,000 worth of jewellery, the time was ripe for a petition to the court presented by Lord Ailesbury, Marjoribanks and others, to remove Harry from the Brewery, referring to their fears that owing to his marriage and inordinately extravagant purchase of jewellery, depositors in the Brewery would lose confidence and withdraw their loans, thus impairing the credit of the firm.

The honeymoon had been delayed but towards the end of the year (1878) the Meuxes set out on a chartered yacht bound for Egypt and the Nile where Harry was to indulge his love of big game hunting. Accompanying them was Walter Ingram, a friend from Harry's time at Cambridge. Valerie's pastime was to purchase antiquities, extending her indulgence to add further objects a few years later, some of which – those that were not fakes – passed eventually to the British Museum.

Either on their outward journey or, more likely, on their return through the Mediterranean, husband and wife stopped at Paris for Louisa Meux to make the acquaintance of her daughter-in law. This was far from being a success. 'I regret very much that I called on her,' Louisa wrote to her brother. 'I have *paid* for Harry's marrying that woman.' And again: 'What a *cruel* way Harry has behaved to us all and what a shameful thing of this woman's to have got such control over him. I wonder they dont pass an act of Parliament to prevent these dreadful cases happening.'[106]

5

Whistler's Portraits

Early the next year the court case was settled, a compromise having been reached by which Harry undertook not to nominate a partner in the Brewery without Marjoribanks's permission – a not so subtle indication of the fear of whom the partner might be – while Lord Ailesbury and Marjoribanks, as Harry's trustees, were allowed sufficient money from Sir Henry's estate to enable Harry to buy and furnish No. 41 Park Lane as his London home. Meanwhile he and Val established themselves in Wiltshire while Marjoribanks was sufficiently well endowed to acquire Brook House for himself and to build on the site. Brook House, Park Lane, rose to five floors and stretched to a succession of ornate reception rooms where he hung his prized Boucher and Fragonard paintings and housed his collection of early Wedgwood. In 1902 it was said 'There is no need for dwellers in Brook House to dream that they dwell in marble halls. They do dwell in them. They realise what the poet merely imagined.'[107] Lord Tweedmouth, as he had become in 1881, also owned an estate, Guisachen, near Beauly, in Inverness.

Among the many investments carried out for the Brewery by Sir Henry Meux's trustees was the 1877 Wiltshire purchase of 50,000 acres of parkland, Dauntsey Manor House (four miles from Wootton Bassett), its stables and a three-acre lake. The original twelfth-century house had been held from Malmesbury Abbey by the Dauntseys until confiscated at the Reformation. Restored to the Crown in the late seventeenth century, it passed through various hands including those of the Earl of Peterborough who enlarged it, adding a plain Georgian front in Bath stone and a long balustraded terrace bordering the slowly gliding River Avon below. At the back, four bays and a venetian window give distinction to an otherwise unexceptional house. Here then was the country domain in which Val selected to launch herself on a Society unwilling to receive her. It was appropriate – since her husband was a keen rider to hounds and she herself a fine horsewoman (perhaps an achievement acquired when under the protection of some other former lover) – this was hunting country, covered part by the Vale of the White Horse Hunt and part by the Duke of Beaufort's. At Dauntsey too Val eventually kennelled her pack of hounds.

Her local obligations, which she enjoyed, extended to the children of the village school: concerts, picnic teas, Christmas entertainments were the conventional formula. Her husband occupied himself with civic duties in the county, serving in the Royal Wiltshire Yeomanry as captain (honorary major), subsequently as honorary lieutenant-colonel; and being appointed magistrate and later High Sheriff for Wiltshire in 1886. His particular interest lay in his excavation of tumuli, known since Domesday and perhaps of Late Neolithic date, in the village of Avebury, celebrated for its enormous stone circle. His enthusiasm gained him a three-year presidency of the Wiltshire Archaeological Society; perhaps he was encouraged by the hope of discoveries to add to his wife's collection of antiquities.[108]

For all her benevolent occupations Val was not achieving

what she most intensely desired – recognition within Wilt-shire Society. The London house too, in Park Lane, should have proved a good launching pad for social advancement but Val failed to convince Society of her respectability. Faced with indifference and being unwilling to blush unseen, she decided to obtain celebrity in the most ostentatious manner that money could buy. She would have her portrait painted by Whistler who had been obliged to leave England a bankrupt in 1879 after his notorious court case of Whistler versus Ruskin. His credit as a painter had not recovered and on his return to London a year later his studio at 13 Tite Street saw few sitters.

Harry Meux commissioned three full-length portraits from Whistler and by early 1881 the first was nearly completed: *Arrangement in Black. Lady Meux.*[109] Val in her luxuriant fur and diamonds and vulgarity, the amplitude of her corseted figure well concealed by the ostentatious flaunting of the magnificently showy cloak, looks out defiantly; her cheeks are flushed with *papier poudre* highlighting the deep violet of her eyes. The jewels on display are those bought for £10,000 by her husband soon after their marriage, being impressed, so the report goes, 'with the necessity of presenting his wife with jewels worthy of her birth and station'.[110] Sketches for Whistler's 'Beautiful Black Lady' exist and the portrait was hung in the Salon of 1882 as *Portrait de M. Harry-Meu.*

The second whole-length, *Harmony in Pink and Grey*,[112] of the same year, is less commanding in posture though tanta-lising in effect as the train catching the light swirls and shim-mers round her feet; it is one of the artist's most successful portrayals. The silvery grey and delicate rose pink of the dress were tones which appealed to Val. Ten years later, when considering another portrait, she wrote to Whistler

Arrangement in Black, Lady Meux, *by Whistler, 1881*

[125]

Harmony in Pink and Grey, Lady Meux, *by Whistler, 1881*

Harry and Val (centre) in the Highlands

that soft colours would be her choice and that she would want to wear 'something dreamy' if she posed for him again. What she certainly did not wish, presumably a suggestion of Whistler's, was to be painted as 'a Spanish female of the 15th century'.[113]

In the early 1880s between sessions for the portrait, as her figure was moulded by Whistler's brush to conform to the accepted stylishness of the age, Val and her husband spent some weeks deer-stalking at Glen Morriston in the western Highlands. From a photograph taken at the time, where her posture is immediately recognisable as that adopted in *Harmony in Pink and Grey*, we are allowed no illusions about our heroine's monumental presence, translated by the artist's brush into modish proportions.

The third portrait, *Harmony in Crimson and Brown*,

Harry and Val Meux in the Highlands, c. 1881

subsequently abandoned,[114] is known only by its related sketches in which the figure is cloaked in dark sables 'reaching nearly to the feet' and carrying a muff.[115] Although the relationship between Whistler and Valerie Meux seems to have been a close one – 'You and I', she wrote, 'always get on well together. I suppose we are a little eccentric and *not* loved by *all* the world'[116] – they nevertheless irritated each other to distraction. In the case of the *Crimson and Brown* portrait, sittings could only take place in the winter as the furs would be packed away during the warm months. Otherwise, unwilling to stand long hours under the weight of the coat, she would sometimes send Alice, her maid, to do duty for her. In July 1886, the picture still unfinished, Whistler was receiving notes from Valerie complaining that she wanted the picture completed as she was having her furs altered; there was also a

dress which she wished returned as it was about to be made
into a cloak. Whereupon Whistler wrote to the effect that he
was leaving London and could no longer struggle with
'melting maids in altered furs' and would prefer to pay back
the money already received and perhaps paint quite a new
arrangement.[117] Finally, one of the last sittings culminated in
Val losing her temper and rounding on him: 'See here, Jimmy
Whistler, you keep a civil tongue in that head of yours or I
will have in someone to *finish* those portraits you made of
me.'[118]

6

Death in Grosvenor Square

Despite the anomaly of birth and of other considerations besides, there are indications that Val had possibly gained some shifting ground with one or two members of Harry's family. Not with the female members however, for in late 1880 Lord Henry Bruce (Harry's uncle) received a letter from his wife, then abroad, of a disapproving tone: 'I did not know you called Mrs Meux by her Christian name.'[119] A year later Lord Ailesbury himself dined at Dauntsey though here any hopes of reconciliation must have been deliberately dashed by his alluding to her only a short time after as an impostor. Lord Henry's attitude may have been founded on the hope that as Harry was and always would be subservient to his strong-minded wife, and since his own sister, Lady Louisa Meux, had recently refused to pay so much as his own Carlton Club entrance fee (adding fatuously and unanswerably: 'If you were not the third son of a younger son you might expect to be better off'), a more cordial relationship with his niece by marriage might pay financial dividends.

Meanwhile, Lady Louisa in Switzerland or France, never mind which as she was inevitably and relentlessly on the move in search of health in the wake of some unknown prognosis, was complaining, making trouble and bemoaning the lack of consideration from her family. 'Why don't my father try to get me a divorce and let me get a husband as the life here is killing me? I was drugged to death last year for *nine* months to get any sleep, it really is dreadful having to live *alone*, my position is quite dreadful.'

Believing that she was being swindled outright by her doctors (which she probably was) and having to recompense the two who came to her in Paris with £600 'and even their *dirty Hotel* bills which they left me to pay', she was unwilling to assist her brothers who were constant in their pecuniary demands of a wealthy sister. Instead, she took every opportunity of voicing some past 'scandalous abuse' by her mother 'whose disgraceful conduct and *infamous* treatment to me at Neuilly' made her own position so unfortunate on the Continent. Once started on her grievances, and they were many, she was insatiable. Her mother had once told her she was 'the *curse* of the whole family' and 'a worthless woman' while her father was aloof and cold. She declared she was living in 'dirty pot houses in Paris' where she had been grossly insulted and called 'a *sale vache*' by the landlord who then turned her out. Her maid said 'que je n'étais qu'une putain', while the one at Lucerne named her a '*singe habillée*'. In Switzerland too she was cursed as a 'damned old bitch and a damned old whore' by some 'vagabonds'.[120] Her family may well have wondered who was the more advanced in lunacy, Sir Henry Meux living out his life in oblivion in Grosvenor Square and East Sheen House in Surrey, or his wife in her shabby life of fantasy and distortion, for there was no reason why she need live abroad. Hers was a case of mental deterioration to which drink and a slanderous tongue had now added further hazards.

Aware of her notorious behaviour in Paris where he was with Louisa Crabbe, John Downes Rochfort wrote as an old friend to Lord Ailesbury.[121] The content can be deduced by the reply which it prompted, not by the recipient but by his wife, who instructed Lord Henry to see that Harry Meux attend to the matter. 'Mr Rochfort should be asked for an explanation' and if, as he told Lady Louisa, 'she ought to be hanged', which the Ailesburys seemed to think an exaggeration (though not impossible), steps should be taken to prevent it, even if it was to have her shut up if there was any good cause for it.

> I suspect that Mr Rochfort is a fast man [Lady Ailesbury continued] and that probably Mrs Crabbe was jealous of his attentions to Louisa. She was *perfectly sane* when I saw her in Paris and in her letter to me she said something of Mr R making a convenience of her by asking for a place in her Opera Box. I have no doubt Mrs C made every convenience of her.

Lady Ailesbury, who one can assume was never her admirer or approved of the irregularity of her life, may have been correct in assuming that Rochfort's letter reflected Louisa Crabbe's jealousy, though more realistically Lady Louisa's behaviour in Paris was such that it needed some disciplinary action to be taken and Rochfort had merely exaggerated his phrasing. Lady Louisa acted in character in believing the Rochforts were presuming on their friendship to obtain the Opera box; perhaps, too, the Rochforts were acting in theirs.

The third day of January 1883 saw Valerie Meux enter into her inheritance – a title, property and a fortune. For over twenty years Sir Henry had existed under the care of doctors, the Arabin family and a household of servants. In the latter years Lord Ailesbury had been down to East Sheen and had seen the patient.

It was impossible to imagine a greater wreck or a more melancholy spectacle than he was. Sir Henry seems utterly incapable of moving in any way; he lies on the sofa and is supported entirely by liquids, taking no solids whatsoever. The medical men are in constant attendance upon him, taking turns in the same way besides other persons who are about him and the establishment numbers some 35 attendants and servants.

And now he was dead. The square were he had lived at No. 36, on the south side, and from where he had shuffled off his unhappy life, was built in 1727 and had held out against businessmen for more than a century and a quarter – poor Sir Henry was not considered as such, simply a lunatic. Although in 1876 it could still be said that there was not a 'plebeian *professional* man living there', two years later a physician, Charles D. T. Phillips, M.D. was emboldened to reside at No. 2. The Meux house was sold and from report 'the fixtures were unusually valuable'.[122]

The new Lady Meux, the forceful partner in the four-year-old marriage, was now in command not only of the new Sir Henry Meux, 3rd Baronet, a pleasant enough man with little ambition beyond an easy life, but also over the increased affluence the termination of her father-in-law's life would bring. As might be expected, they were displeased with the new direction of the Brewery management in which the Trust was brought to an end and though all assets and half the profits were Henry's, he was deprived of the authority of running the firm's policies. The generous provision for his mother was continued. There was also an on-going struggle in which Lord Tweedmouth made a reappearance and in which Henry – and no need to seek for Val's determined egging-on – wished to bring a case concerning an earlier restrictive financial transaction. As there was no support for this argument no action was taken.

A very few days after the death in Grosvenor Square a curious incident arose between Val and Lord Henry Bruce. The women on his side of the family were still hostile but relations between Val and young Henry's uncle had improved to the point that he offered her a piece of jewellery of her own choice from Messrs Hancocks, the family jeweller in Bruton Street, for which he would pay. Whether it was to make ground with the Meuxes with a calculating eye to pecuniary favours to come, or whether Lord Henry had been captivated by Val's undeniable good looks and engaging outward manner it is not possible to do more than conjecture. At the same time and in return, Val was to reward this gesture with a pair of cufflinks.

Signing herself 'Yours affectionately' she despatched the following letter to him on 8 January 1883:

I have chosen the Diamond Buckle and told Hancocks to send you the account, price £500. I must thank you very much, and have ordered the sleeve-links to be sent to you. With our love and once more thanking you for this kind present . . .

Opposition of some kind must have arisen at 36 Eaton Place, Lord Henry's house (within a few doors of Rochfort and No. 42). Could the arrival of a pair of cufflinks have been observed by his wife, together with the letter from Hancocks?

36 Bruton Street [9 January 1883]
My Lord, We beg respectfully herewith to enclose for your Lordship as requested an account for a diamond

buckle, £500, chosen by Lady Meux yesterday and taken away by her Ladyship.

The tale of profligacy disclosed, did Lady Henry oblige her husband, at her instruction, to write to the jewellers?

In reply to your letter of the 9th Inst., no-one would be more happy than myself to give my Niece Lady Bruce Meux such a handsome present as a Diamond Buckle of the value of £500, but I regret extremely to say I am not in a position to do so, if fact to be candid my wife Lady Henry has *not* got £500 worth of Diamonds *all told* – nothing like it. Kindly explain this to Her Ladyship and at the same time express to her my *deep regret* that I am unable, *through no fault of mine,* to comply with her wishes.[123]

Perhaps the whole thing was a lark to needle Lady Henry and the last few words seem to imply some mutual understanding between the protagonists. Remembering that Val was a very Croesus compared to the man who even now was appealing to his aged father for money (thus eliciting a reply from his mother: 'Cannot you wait as we did and leave us enough to live on for the short time we shall want it'), the incident remains perplexing.

7

Dolly Tester

In Paris Louisa had more domestic upheavals, more wearisome complaints to her brother that a maid had tried to drive her 'to throw myself into the *Seine*'. She had now drifted to Mentone but her conduct in Paris had proved quite unmanageable and poor Lord Henry was appealed to by a friend of hers. The news that he had to tell on 5 April 1885 was that Louisa had 'got into a most wretched, disgraceful squabble on the racecourse' and was in such a perilously excited state that the police commissary were called and an English 'gentleman horsedealer' by the name of Walker – (a thorough rogue) – with whom she was acquainted, endeavoured to quieten her or else the police would have removed her from the course – whereupon Louisa turned upon Mr Walker and 'abused him without measure' and accused him of robbing her 'etc., etc., etc.' Walker, whose 'gentlemanly' attributes shone more advantageously in the horsedealing line, had been thus arraigned before; now urged by his patrons he was determined to take steps to clear his character and was claiming £800 damages. He had legal right to take civil proceedings for damages and also to have her Ladyship up before the 'correctional police' who had the power, which they would probably use, to send her to prison as she had been cautioned and had neglected several warnings. She had been urged to leave

France at once or else settle with Walker for the sum of £50 or £100.[124]

Before this most unfortunate drunken episode, the Ailesburys, then at their Villa Marbella, Biarritz, had received information that their daughter, was creating disturbances in Paris. Afraid, now that her husband was dead, she would marry anybody she pleased, they entreated Lord Henry to travel to Paris and give her some good advice. They feared she might marry 'that *fearful* man or fall into the hands of some adventurer'.[125]

The report received of her misbehaviour and state of health was such that Henry Meux was written to and begged to go to his mother in Mentone where, as we have seen, she had gone to 'try a change of air', her doctor accompanying her. This he did 'like a *dear good* boy' (so his grandparents agreed) on his way to his yacht at Marseilles, and 'a charming fellow' his mother thought him. By the following year dispositions had been made that with £10,000 a year from the Meux fortune Lord Henry would be in charge of his sister and would find her a house with a resident doctor and two women in attendance and a large garden. It had been resolved that having reached 'a certain period of life' she must be taken care of. And there we leave Lady Louisa Meux who died in her Paris house, rue Gallilée in 1896, leaving all her property to her son.

With the prospect of Louisa being settled, the aged Ailesburys may have hoped to spend their declining years undisturbed by the wranglings of a singularly inharmonious family. (Lord Ailesbury at least had the solace of his regular visits to 'Mother Crabbe' at Sidmouth Lodge, enhanced by his flirtation with the beautiful Midge.) But if so they were soon to be undeceived.

Lord Ailesbury had had four sons; the eldest, George, had died in Ajaccio in 1868 leaving a boy, William ('dear Willie'), aged five to be brought up by a wayward mother and by the child's Ailesbury grandparents. Though fond, as they had been of Harry Meux, and well-disposed, they were hardly exemplary guardians – witness the conduct of their own children, forever quarrelling with their parents. In fact George, with his spiteful tongue, used to refer to his mother, whom he disliked, as 'Bellone, the goddess of war and discord'.[126]

Lacking any parental discipline, 'dear Willie', bearing the courtesy title of Viscount Savernake, grew into a little monster. His tastes were of the lowest and leaving Eton 'under a cloud' he gleaned his associates from the stable yard and the tavern. For preference he dressed in the pearly attire of a costermonger and, moreover, spoke as one.[127] Expelled for life from the Jockey Club for fraud relating to the running of a horse, by the time he reached his majority he was in debt for £185,000. It was said of him that 'his mind was a dunghill of which his tongue was the cock'.[128]

Val did not find the disreputable society in which he moved altogether alien, though she professed to having tried to dissuade him from mixing in it. Besides, she enjoyed his company. The Ailesburys, unaware, perhaps intentionally so, of the disgrace to which Willie's habits had led him, were indignant that she might exert a bad influence on the young aristocrat. Some kind of rumour of which we only know the substance was going the round: that Val would kill her husband and marry Lord Savernake, heir to Lord Ailesbury and his estates. No doubt it was Willie who circulated this scandalous accusation so as to activate discord among all parties, following it up by informing Val that Lady Ailesbury was the perpetrator of the charge. Val lost no time in counter-attacking:

> Even your rank and age does not entitle you to bring against me the base accusation you have. I don't understand so much about murder as evidently you do. I only hope that when I am so near the grave as you are that I shall not be half so uncharitable. The only reason you have to be so spiteful towards me is that I am your grandson's wife. You must own that I have behaved better towards him than his Mother did to his Father. I can very honestly say that my sins were committed before marriage and not after. You seem to forget that you put yourself in the power of the Lord by saying that I will kill my husband and marry Lord Savernake. It is a terrible thing to say even about your bitterest enemy. I like Lord Savernake but not in the way you think I do. There is a great deal of good in him and all my friends are of the same opinion. I have done my best to try and make him drop his London acquaintances. It is only kindness that can do this, not bullying.[129]

The Ailesburys had been inconvenienced by so many family disturbances in their lives that this last imputation does not seem to have provoked them unduly, though Lord Ailesbury referred to it when writing to Lord Henry:

> *Val* has written *unprovoked* the *most insulting* letter to your mother I ever read. Of course it is not written by herself as she can scarcely spell her own *name*. Your mother has very properly sent the letter back to the kiddy [Henry Meux] and of course *not replied* to

it. What can have made her do it I cannot possibly conceive as your mother has never written to her in her life. I suspect Master Willie.[130]

There was worse to follow. Lord Ailesbury's diary for 10 May 1884 provides this information:

Heard first from Robert [his son] which I did not believe the dreadful news that Willie was married to a Prostitute.

There was no Louisa Crabbe at The Boltons to run down to in a carriage for sympathy as she and Rochfort were at their Villa Philippe, Monte Carlo. On 12 May the diary has a conclusive tale to tell:

Alas! Alas! It is true. Perfectly overwhelmed with grief. All true and utterly hopeless.

Willie had fought for and won the affections of the barmaid of the Theatre Royal, Brighton. True to form he had defeated an opponent for her favours in a pugilistic bout at the back of the stands of the Portsmouth racecourse and had married her at the Registry Office, St George's Street, Hanover Square, London, where he gave his age as twenty-one, his profession as cab proprietor, of Kendal's Mews, George Street, Marylebone.[131]

Dolly Tester of the halls, when 'resting' from her sprightly exertions in pantomime – she was remembered as Jinbad the Jailer in the 1879 Christmas *Sinbad the Sailor*[132] at Brighton and had more recently appeared in the chorus at the Empire and elsewhere – would offer her attractions in the refreshment department of Brighton's Theatre Royal. But she was a good creature of a kind and had more merit than her worthless husband, who having settled her in a house on the Savernake estate a few miles from Dauntsey, continued to frequent the racecourses and to associate with his many undesirable cronies.

Meanwhile Val Meux at close-by Dauntsey was preparing to give Lady Savernake some disciplinary advice regarding the comportment fitting for a potential peeress. (A sure case of the pot calling the kettle black.) Elevated to the position of a future marchioness (and how near that future was), Doll, whose real name was Julia Hasely, of very humble parentage, resented any patronising from one whose career had been as informal as her own, so that on Val driving the few miles from Dauntsey House to Christian Malford to implement her preaching, she was told to her disgust that Lady Savernake was 'not at home', a harmless enough phrase but one that could be taken as a sure way of expressing an unwillingness to see the visitor. Injured and insulted, so the story goes, Val proceeded to break every window close enough for her umbrella or a stone to reach.

Willie's was a wasted life. When he died in 1894 at Brixton in the house of his estate agent, having succeeded his grandfather eight years earlier, the local press, alluding to the 'follies of the young marquess', gave him a phlegmatic obituary. 'As a peer', it read, 'he had savoured the incense of a multitude of toadies', and referred to the £200,000 owing to the moneylender who had encouraged the near-fateful sale of the Savernake 40,000-acre estate to Sir Edward Guinness (Lord Iveagh, 'the Irish merchant') for three quarter of a million pounds. This cruel intention of Willie's, for in 800 years Savernake had never been bought or sold, had been fought through the courts, and won by his uncle and heir, Lord Henry, and the trustees.[133] Doll,

Dowager Marchioness, made a more conventional second marriage to a JP of Arbroath, Forfar.

8

Theobalds

In the last two years since Sir Henry Meux's death in 1883, the interior of Theobalds Park had undergone a thorough transformation. It had not been lived in during his disturbed lifetime and now, while still enjoying a style of life in Park Lane (a much sought-after address though towards the end of the century it began to assume a '*nouveau riche*' tone), the Meuxes decided to settle at Theobalds in spite of their tenure of Dauntsey. Perhaps the latter was a shade too close to Savernake estate for unimpeded pleasure, though what entertaining Val foresaw it would have been hard to say, since aristocracy and gentry, especially within the female contingent, ignored her. But with confidence and determination to gain her ends things soon took on a lively turn.

Theobalds in Hertfordshire, or 'Tibbalds' as pronounced in the past and always so by Valerie, was first mentioned in 1441 as an early manor house. In 1583 the great Lord Burghley, chief minister in Queen Elizabeth's reign, built his palace half a mile north of the old dwelling. The princely house stood in the manner of St James's Palace around two courts, enhanced by lakes and pleasure gardens and a deer park for hunting. On Burghley's death the estate passed to his son Sir Robert Cecil, 1st Earl of Salisbury. King James I, the owner of Hatfield Manor, also in Hertfordshire, persuaded

Cecil to exchange houses with him. When this was effected in 1607 Lord Salisbury began the building of Hatfield House. The King's twenty-year occupancy of Theobalds was marked by the menagerie he assembled of white falcons, flying squirrels and white hind. When death claimed him there in 1625 it was at the palace gates that the Knight Marshal proclaimed Charles Prince of Wales as King of England, Scotland, France and Ireland. Thereafter Theobalds was pillaged and all but destroyed during the Commonwealth.

In the second half of the eighteenth century, half a mile to the west of the earlier palace, a large red brick three-storey pedimented house rose with a forward-curving one-storey colonnade on either side leading to small outer wings which in turn looked towards the sweep of the drive and the porticoed entrance to the house.

With the arrival of the Meuxes the house was again enlarged to meet the requirements of a wealthy and pretentious woman whose aim was to impress. The space behind the colonnades had already been filled in and now a larger conservatory was added, while on the north side a five-storey tower rose up, of neo-Renaissance appearance, which added very considerably to the number of bedrooms, afforded a capacious kitchen, a gun room and other amenities, and housed the water tanks. A Turkish bath was added to the house, and there was roller-skating for those who wished to go 'rinking'. The garden front looked onto a peaceful stretch of parkland encompassing ancient trees and an ornamental lake formed by the New River. Here, on a small island to the north-east (with perhaps the enthusiasm of the former monarch), Henry installed his menagerie of emus and ostriches and other unlikely birds.

Valerie now had space enough to arrange the trophies

Theobalds Park, Hertfordshire

The garden side

bought on her two visits to Egypt and to form a museum
with the exhibits which she valued highly. Pride of place was
given to the mummy bought by its new owner from Walter
Ingram who had accompanied the Meux honeymooners to
the Nile in 1879 and had more recently joined the relief
expedition to Khartoum in the ill-fated attempt to save
General Gordon. Bought by Ingram from an Arab, the
mummy was said to carry a curse relating to the hieroglyphics
on the coffin, to the effect that anyone associated with it
would die childless and undergo a gruesome death.[134] Val
was delighted with her purchase which rose in celebrity when
the curse appeared to have come good by the death of
Ingram, married but childless, gored to death while elephant
shooting at Berber in 1888.

Her interests were not confined to the museum where the
objects would grow in quantity and in value. Money she had
and a magnificent house; moreover, her looks were unim-
paired. Still the head of resplendent golden brown hair and
the large eyes of dazzling violet. But though young-looking
for her age, 'her figure was ungainly and had become more
so. Seated at table Lady Meux was a pleasure to the eye. On
her feet – she was grotesque.' 'Never in my life have I seen
one of her sex compare with her as a trencherwoman. "Ever
seen Lady Meux wolf potatoes?"'[135] With a vitality that
never failed she launched herself into entertaining on a lavish
scale, but her self-assurance faltered in the company of those
she most wanted to impress; so that she set her sights first on
the tenantry and local tradespeople, inviting them to the
coach house for evenings of eating and drinking, carousing
until the early hours, herself rather than Henry responding to
the toasts given by the guests to their hosts. But she would
have nothing to do with her neighbours for fear of being

patronised. She neither gambled nor drank; her preference was for young men and practical jokes. As an example of the combination of these preferences, a young male sycophant undertook for a wager to swing from hanging rope to hanging rope, the length of the swimming pool. As one rope had been purposely rendered defective in the middle it was no surprise when an immersion in full evening dress was the finale to that buffoonery.

As Valerie's domination in the household increased, Henry played less part in his wife's eccentricities. Slowly, but by incontrovertible degrees, the bottle became his chief companion. At weekends when the house was filled with new and largely unknown faces (Val 'liked a kaleidoscope'),[136] when pranks, consumption of drink, gaiety of a sort, and fights in the billiard room were the order, Theobalds was likened by one visitor to R. S. Surtees's Nonsuch House where the Scattercashes welcomed near-strangers, entertaining freely and opulently,[137] though at Theobalds no women were invited.

There were awkward scenes as when Valerie voiced some inaccuracy and Henry gently observed: 'But do you think so, my dear, because I remember . . . ' and was cut short, 'Oh! For God's sake, Harry, shut up thrusting your oar in at every moment.' At this Henry's patience gave way and he swore like a trooper, whereupon Val, summoning Smith, butler and despot at Theobalds, ordered him to 'speak to Sir Henry'.[138] It was this same Smith who would watch with a cynical flicker of the eye while three liveried footmen placed plates of food on the floor for the fox terriers.

There were tales in abundance concerning the conduct of the mistress of the house and her guests. These arose from a report that all the many bedrooms had communicating doors and that each room bore its own symbolic name, thus:

Antony, Cleopatra, Helen, Paris, Bathsheba and so on –
Aphrodite was considered most apt for a bathroom. Elsewhere in the house there were bedrooms presupposing a
change of behaviour – the Nunnery, the Confessional, Lady
Abbess's Room, the Anchorite's Cell; the Virgin's Room
boasted 'a massive brass bedstead'.

How Val must have enjoyed this flouting of convention
which was her way of responding to Society's criticism of her.

Two newcomers joined the household at about this time,
Arthur Lambton as secretary at Theobalds and Miss Margaret
McMillan at Park Lane. Both have left descriptions of the
principal characteristics of the woman who sought to rule
their public and private lives.

In 1888 Margaret McMillan,[139] of Scottish parentage
from Inverness, educated at Inverness High School, and
Academy, was sent through an agency to 41 Park Lane. A
woman of twenty-nine and a staunch socialist, she had done
voluntary work with her sister for the Labour Movement and
before that had been governess and a student teacher in
Geneva and Lausanne. Now she needed paid work to
implement her precarious livelihood. Presenting herself at
Park Lane for an interview, of Lady Meux she had never
heard. On arrival, and on being shown by the butler into a
small boudoir all lined in plush, the writing table covered
with heavy silver objects and Whistler's portrait of a woman
in diamonds and black lace hanging on the wall, she was
aware of 'the new and welcome change' from the East End
where she had been working. 'Decked out in her finest
plumage', Val must have been a singular contrast to Margaret's earlier employers. She felt that Val was 'under some
kind of shadow' but could not place it until Val explained
that marriage to Henry was a social scandal, that she was 'a

woman not received' and though distinguished men came to her house, never their women. 'I am outside,' she said and she feared that Margaret might not get another place if she came to her; that it was only right to tell her so but that she wanted her as companion and someone to write her letters, as her own spelling was perfunctory. For her part Margaret was outspoken in her socialist loyalty and asked Val if she too were a socialist. Val replied, 'I a socialist? Look at my rings,' and she held out her hands rich with diamonds sparkling in the glow of the fire, her neck circled with ropes of pearls. 'Socialism is a creed for down-and-outs,' she continued, 'and you will abandon it at once. Besides, it's irreligious.'

But remuneration was high and the rewards many. The very next day Margaret was taken shopping by Val (she had already burned Margaret's hat) and a profusion of clothes were purchased, but although she acknowledged the influence of her new employer and danced to its tune while attending socialist meetings in her fine new clothes (which branded her as a capitalist), she wondered how long she could give satisfaction to someone whose values were so different from her own. She soon became aware of the difficulties inherent in her employment. At the outset she could discuss and argue amicably, but by degrees this led to uncomfortable confrontations. Valerie's entertaining was the quintessence of her own nature. Her guests at dinner were those who needed money for new businesses, to pay off debts, or for other similar requirements. Val, sure of her ground, would act generously, meanwhile extorting a bargain for which she held the cards. That bargain was to act as she pleased. Seated at table watching these people, comfortable now, their requests agreed to, she would lash out at them, contemptuously, stinging, insulting, mocking them, holding them in her power. Her behaviour was outrageous; neverthe-less these same guests, humiliated by their benefactor, would have at least achieved for themselves what they had sought.

Margaret found London preferable to Theobalds, for here at least there was the entertainment of the theatre, shops to visit and purchases to be made, drives to take. But there was no mistaking the fact that all sources of amusement had been used up; Val's powers were wasted 'in remorse, regret and suspicion'. It was hard to keep pace with such a woman; one day Margaret would be praised and overwhelmed with gifts, then dismissed in disgrace. 'Sailing on a mad sea,' she thought, 'storms came from nowhere, then ceased abruptly.'

The final storm blew up on May Day 1892 when Val heard that Margaret had spoken for socialism on a platform in Hyde Park. She was dismissed: 'Well, that's the end. Go! You may blot me out of your memory', and Margaret, still retaining some affection for her erstwhile erratic employer, sacrificed material comforts and returned to work for the Labour Movement. Later she made a remarkable career in education, introducing health centres for children and other analogous work. Before her death in 1931 she had been invested with the Order of the Companions of Honour.

Arthur Lambton's position at Theobalds was that of private secretary to Henry, as least that was the post offered him and which he accepted at £10 a week. Before long he realised, first, that he was underpaid, and furthermore that he had not been engaged to fulfil secretarial duties but to keep his employer away from his wife, 'the wrecker of his career'. Henry's propensity for drink had assumed abnormal propor-tions, while his guests often also imbibed too freely. There was an occasion at dinner when one of the company over-balanced his chair, subsiding transversely, partly on the fender and partly on the floor, seemingly content to remain there. Arthur Lambton reported the incident: 'To my dying day I shall never forget the insouciance with which the footmen stepped over his prostrate form, handing the dishes to the unheeding guests.'[140]

Eventually Lambton decided life had become intolerable at Theobalds what with the company, the vulgarity on display, Henry's drinking, Val's insults. To remain would be to lose all self-respect. He left quite suddenly one afternoon. Valerie had overheard him suggest to the man who was marking the score at a game of real tennis that when the game was finished they might have one together, 'Pretty good thing, if one's servants are to play tennis whenever they think of it,' she remarked. He paid no farewell but took his departure within the half hour.

9

Temple Bar

A distraction of some importance to the Meuxes – and engineered by Valerie – occurred in 1888, adding importance to Theobalds.

Christopher Wren's Temple Bar, a stone gateway of 1670 adjoining the Temple and defining the limits of the Strand with Fleet Street, had been removed from its site in 1878 allowing further space for G. E. Street's grandiose Royal Courts of Justice and thus enabling the widening of the street. When the gateway had been dismantled the stones had lain disregarded in a rough yard off the Farringdon Road. In the late 1880s the Court of Common Council and the Lands Committee were still considering where best to erect the gateway when by some unexplained action (though probably by offering to pay), more on Val's part than on her husband's, the Court of Common Council voted, though not unanimously, that the Meuxes should have this historic structure erected on their own property, thus presenting a magnificent park entrance to an already notable house.

Four hundred tons of stonework were removed to Theobalds where in early January 1888 a glass jar containing coins and a newspaper were placed beneath the foundation stone laid by Valerie. By September of the same year the great Wren gateway, with the room above the central arch

Temple Bar erected at Theobalds in 1888

embellished with 'Spy' cartoons from *Vanity Fair*, had found a new home.

Henry had the gratification of witnessing this enhancement to his property but there was little life left for him to enjoy. Drink had debilitated him and his wife's indifference and galling contempt had reduced his life to a meaningless shadow. Death released him on 11 January 1900 with few to mourn him and Val to inherit a fortune. His coffin when interred in the Cheshunt family vault was smothered in a profusion of his widow's wreaths.

As an act of commemoration she presented Dauntsey Parish Church with a stained-glass east window of three lights, the centre one incorporating the likeness of a saint crowned and armed with an unsheathed sword while,

[153]

curiously, sporting a pair of earrings. The face and figure carry a strange resemblance to Valerie herself.

In 1899, while Henry was eking out the last semblance of life, England was watching with dismay the losses inflicted on her army by the Boers in the South African War. In late October Captain the Hon. Hedworth Lambton in command of the cruiser *Powerful* arrived at Durban with a naval brigade and a battery of two 4.7 inch naval guns and four 12-pounders. Proceeding to Ladysmith in command of the naval brigade he helped relieve the siege. On his arrival at Portsmouth early the next year he was greeted as the hero of the hour.

Val's patriotism was aflame, counterbalanced only by her desire to meet the man who had covered himself in glory. Her ardour in sending out six naval 12-pounder guns to Lord Roberts, Commander-in-Chief in South Africa, brought Captain Lambton to thank her for so generous an act. The handsome, aristocratic hero bowled her over. This third son of the 2nd Earl of Durham was now forty-four years old and carried with his birthright all the dash and self-confidence of a man gaining the top of his profession. Val had always had an eye for younger men but for her this last obsession was to have no competitors. Earlier in this volume he has been introduced in Athens in 1889 under another guise. His prowess in seduction was as felicitous as his seamanship and when in charge on the China Station he had carried on an impressive love affair with the German Minister's wife even to soliciting her successfully to stay on board his flagship.[141] But paramount in his affections was Viscountess Chelsea, as were her children, one in particular. Valerie had let Temple House on the Theobalds estate to the family, liking them better than her neighbours, thus ensuring herself regular

contact with Vice-Admiral Lambton (as he had now become),
who married Lady Chelsea in 1910 two years after the death
of her husband.

10

Gain and Loss

Val's energies did not diminish with age and were now directed towards the Turf. Racing was to be her new absorption. For some years a stud had existed at Crews Hill on the Theobalds estate and it was there that Sefton, the 1878 Derby winner belonging to Stirling Crawford, had been bred. By the end of that year the stud had been bought jointly by him and Henry Chaplin, the noted sportsman and politician.

However, it was some years later that Val, under the name of 'Mr Theobald', established her own stud in buildings just outside the gates and registered her colours, red with a green sash. She was more inclined to lease horses and in 1900 there had been no end of a dispute resulting in a lawsuit. Her two-year-old colt Volodyovski (happily pronounced 'Bottle o' Whisky' by backers), had been leased to Lord William Beresford, husband of the Duke of Marlborough's widow who at Beresford's death chose to claim that the lease automatically passed to her. Val claimed otherwise; so did Mr Justice Grantham who contended that the lease of a racehorse was a personal thing and would be vested only where the owner had full confidence; when death supervened the lease would end.

Following this satisfactory outcome Volodyovski was leased to W. C. Whitney, American millionaire, sportsman

Lady Meux with Volodyovski, 1901

and one-time Secretary of the Navy in President Cleveland's administration. His colours were carried by the American jockey Lester Reiff, an extremely able rider. On 5 June 1901, with the betting 5-2 on, Volodyovski won the Derby by three-quarters of a length in a field of twenty-five.[142] To have one's horse win the Derby was not only gratifying but irrepressibly exciting for Val who took all the plaudits in the paddock to herself even though Volodyovski had run under another's colours.

By the beginning of the 1900s the Meux Brewery, until then so prosperous, showed a depreciation in its shares owing in part to the Brewery being over a hundred years old and in need of a new site, also to the depression in the aftermath of the Boer War. Brook House, then the property of the first Lord Tweedmouth's son, was sold in 1906 and became the home of Sir Ernest Cassel and subsequently of his granddaughter, Edwina Mountbatten. Valerie was also hit financially, but simply sold the major part of her Wiltshire property as she gaily set her course from one extravagance to another.

In search of health she journeyed abroad in the latter part of 1901. Returning to London on 19 December, she put up at the Coburg Hotel, Carlos Place, Grosvenor Square, intending to reach Theobalds at lunchtime the following day. But in the night death extinguished that tough, designing veteran. Her death certificate gave the cause of death as cirrhosis of the liver and dropsy and her age as 'about 63 years'; the first and last words were subsequently crossed out. On 30 December her impressive oak coffin was laid alongside that of her husband in the family vault in Cheshunt's parish churchyard.

Her will, made at the start of the year, was a formal declaration of the bitterness which had never healed towards her husband's family. In leaving them a very small proportion of her riches she gave as her reason 'the omission on their part and on the part of their respective families to receive me as the wife of my late husband and as such as a member of the family and by reason of the omission to show a proper sense of gratitude for the benefits conferred upon them by me during my life time'. Those to whom she felt some stirring of friendliness were remembered, sometimes on the quaintest of conditions. The young Lord George Cholmondeley, for instance, was to receive £3,000 'providing he married a lady in society' – which he did not. Val's large collection of Egyptian antiquities, consisting of sepulchral figures and vases, bronze figures of gods and the statue of Rameses III King of Egypt, had been catalogued for her in 1898 by Sir William Budge, Keeper of Egyptian and Assyrian antiquities at the British Museum, once a contemporary of Harry Meux at Cambridge. This collection was left to the British Museum under the condition that it should not be separated but placed in a suitable position. It was found impossible to comply with these specifications and was sold at auction in 1911, William Randolph Hearst acquiring many of the objects.

But the astonishing dénouement, awaited with curiosity, was the disclosure of the name of the principal recipient of Val's great wealth. Innumerable wills had been made in the past (so it was said), hopeful young males being named. But here, irrevocably, was the wish that the man who had captured her affections and had held her friendship for the last ten years should benefit. As a constant reminder of his benefactor and on condition that he changed his name to Meux – which he did – the gallant Hedworth Lambton inherited not only Theobalds but a brewer's fortune besides.

SIMPLIFIED AILESBURY FAMILY TREE

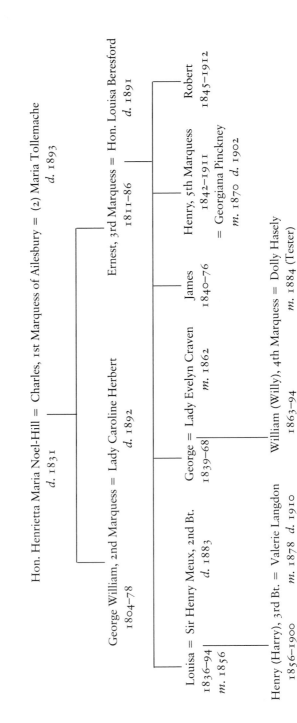

Hon. Henrietta Maria Noel-Hill = Charles, 1st Marquess of Ailesbury = (2) Maria Tollemache
d. 1831   *d.* 1893

George William, 2nd Marquess = Lady Caroline Herbert
1804–78   *d.* 1892

Ernest, 3rd Marquess = Hon. Louisa Beresford
1811–86   *d.* 1891

Louisa = Sir Henry Meux, 2nd Bt.
1836–94   *d.* 1883
m. 1856

George = Lady Evelyn Craven
1839–68   *m.* 1862

James
1840–76

Henry, 5th Marquess = Georgiana Pinckney
1842–1911   *m.* 1870 *d.* 1902

Robert
1845–1912

Henry (Harry), 3rd Bt. = Valerie Langdon
1856–1900   *m.* 1878 *d.* 1910

William (Willy), 4th Marquess = Dolly Hasely
1863–94   *m.* 1884 (Tester)

Notes

1 Terry, Ellen, *The Story of My Life*, 2nd ed., n.d., 63.
2 Barker, Kathleen, 'The Theatre Royal, Bristol', *Society for Theatre Research*, 1974.
3 Surtees, V., ed., *The Diary of Ford Madox Brown*, Yale U.P., 164, 165.
4 *Era, The*, 9 March 1856.
5 Sala, G. A., *Twice Round the Clock*, 248.
6 Sherson, E., *London's Lost Theatres*, 93.
7 *Illustrated London Magazine, The*, 1855, iii, 219.
8 Scott, Clement, *Thirty Years at the Play and Dramatic Table Talk*, 102.
9 Southern, Richard, *Victorian Theatre*, 76.
10 Nicoll, Allardyce, *History of the English Drama*, v, 30.
11 Pemberton, E., *The Life and Writings of T. W. Robertson*, 54.
12 Sherson, 44.
13 Vizetelly, H., *Glances Back through Seventy Years*, i, 426. The Shakespeare Head was the semi-Bohemian meeting place of actors, artists, playwrights of the 'quoting, gripping, quaffing, club' of fellow workers in Bohemia.
14 Colonel Rochfort's first wife, Henrietta, was the daughter of Sir Horace Mann, Bt, British envoy to the Court of Tuscany and close friend of Horace Walpole.
15 Princeton University Library. The sketch head for Mary Magdalene is at the Ashmolean Museum, Oxford; the finished pen and ink drawing at the Fitzwilliam Museum, Cambridge.
16 Surtees, V., ed., *The Diaries of George Price Boyce*, 24.
17 Burne-Jones, G., *Memorials*, i, 186, 187.

18 Cook, E. T. and Wedderburn, A., *The Works of John Ruskin*, xxxvi, 302.
19 Manchester City Art Gallery; Aberdeen City Art Gallery; British Museum; Birmingham City Art Gallery; Tate Gallery, respectively.
20 According to Benezit: On a rapproché [à Swinton] d'avoir exagéré la joliesse anglaise.'
21 MacCarthy, Fiona, *William Morris*, 150.
22 *Memorials*, i, 169.
23 Holograph at the British Library.
24 My sister, E. Bruce, concocted this tale (*The Last American Aristocrat*, N. D. Langford, 1996) and though it would be pleasing to suppose it, in all our discussions over the years this possibility never arose. It makes a good if inaccurate story.
25 Information from Mrs Katharine MacDonald.
26 For this and the following letter: Special Collections and Archives Division, University of British Columbia, Canada.
27 *Memorials*, i, 70.
28 Frith, *Reminiscences*, i, 280-2. A print of the picture given to her by Frith always hung in her room.
29 *The Era*, 17 January 1858.
30 *The Victorian Underworld*, 345.
31 Barton, M., *Garrick*, 67.
32 Private collection.
33 The use of French to describe the softening of the brain was a bow to convention. Making use of a euphemism was less shocking to the family. (Until quite recently a *crise de nerfs* would denote a nervous breakdown.)
34 Hibbert, H. G., *A Playgoer's Memories*.
35 Terry, Ellen, 65.
36 Hunt, Violet, Unpublished diaries.
37 Coleman, J., *Charles Reade*, 203.
38 Trevelyan, Pauline Lady, Unpublished diaries, 19 January 1861.
39 Scott, C., *Thirty Years at the Play*, 83.
40 Ellis, S. M., *A Mid-Victorian Pepys*, 152.
41 Hay, C., *The Club and the Drawing Room*, ii, 192.
42 Robertson, T. W., 90.

43 Information from the late Kathleen Barker.
44 *Survey of London*, XLI. Much help, patiently given by Mr P. A.
Bezodis to the author who remembers the gate posts just before
the Second World War but the house had gone and the present
Telephone Exchange was about to be built (1939).
45 Victoria and Albert Museum, Print Room, 96.A.10.
46 Stirling, A. M. W., *A Painter of Dreams*, 299.
47 Mrs Rosalind Pulver in 'Who Was J. D. Rochfort?', *Antique
Dealer and Collector's Guide*, January 1993, quoted from G. W.
and F. A. Rhead, *Staffordshire Pots and Potters*.
48 Information from Dr Frankie Morris. Mrs Pulver has told me
that Mary, another daughter of J. B. Tenniel, eventually
married C. G. Green, a Derbyshire potter, 'after a stormy
courtship'. Perhaps another misalliance.
49 Engen, R., *John Tenniel's Alice's White Knight*, 2.
50 *The Graphic*, 31 December 1864.
51 Green, R. Lancelyn, *Diaries of Lewis Carroll*, i, 230.
52 Wallack, Lester, *Memories of Fifty Years*, 48
53 *Thirty Years at the Play*, 78-80.
54 Theatre Museum Collection. The play had its first production
at the Surrey Theatre, 5 February 1866. It is just possible that
Miss Herbert is referring to Ouida's novel *Idalia*.
55 Anson, P. F., *Fashions in Church Furniture*, 209.
56 Burnand, ii, 372.
57 Irving, Laurence, *Henry Irving, The Actor and His World*,
132-3.
58 Duncan, Barry, *The St James's Theatre*, 128.
59 Bigland, Eileen, *Ouida*, 45.
60 The following account is taken from *The St James's Theatre*,
130-2.
61 This and the folowing letter are quoted by permission of the
Maslin Collection, Shakespeare Centre Library, Stratford-
upon-Avon.
62 Laurence Irving to the author.
63 University of British Columbia, Canada.
64 Naylor, L. E., *The Irrepressible Victorian*, 11.
65 Information from the late Mr Anthony Butler, Mrs Butler, and

also from Mr Maldwin Drummond's correspondence with the author and from his *Salt Water Palaces*.
66 Private collection. Information from Mrs Betty Elzea.
67 Jopling, Louise, *Twenty Years of My Life*, 96-7.
68 Ibid., 91.
69 Ibid., 93.
70 Information from Mrs J. P. Cowpe and Miss Beryl Varley, Royal Brompton Hospital.
71 Bishop, P. J., Lucas, B. D. B., *The Seven Ages of the Brompton*, 41-2.
72 *Survey of London*, XLI, 137.
73 At Christie's South Kensington, 25 April 1996, Lot 83.
74 Delaware Art Museum and Mary Bancroft Memorial Collection.
75 27 November 1880. British Library.
76 Linder, Leslie, *The Journals of Beatrix Potter*, 1966, 44.
77 Ailesbury Archives, Wiltshire. [AW infra.]
78 Ipswich Archives.
79 Boyce *Diaries*. Bought by Colnaghi for £25.4s and by the British Museum that same year for £26.9s.
80 AW.
81 In November 1871 while at Eton Arthur had saved the life of a small child from drowning by diving into the river by the Playing Fields where the current was strong. This was reported in the *Daily Telegraph*. Lord Ernest, having had the information from 'our mutual friend Oscar Browning' at the Mayor's inaugural feast at Windsor, wrote his congratulations to Louisa. He had given Arthur the nickname earlier still.
82 *Survey of London*, XXXIX.
83 'Don't bite your bread. Break it off.' O. B. Bunce, *Don't, A Manual of Mistakes*, 1890.
84 See Part II of this book.
85 Askwith, Betty, *A Victorian Young Lady*, 128.
86 Ibid., 132.
87 Someone with Miss Herbert's name gave lessons in elocution at the Bijou Theatre; she has occasionally been confused with Louisa.

88 *Survey of London*, XL. Coincidentally, the Meux bride-to-be was of the family who lived at Tottenham Park, Savernake, rebuilt by Thomas Cundy the elder. The Upper Brook Street house was rebuilt in 1906.

89 Cardigan, Earl of, *The Wardens of Savernake Forest*, 307-8.

90 Thompson, F. M. L., *England's Landed Society in the 19th century*, 190, 260.

91 *The Complete Peerage.*

92 Information from Michael Meredith, School Librarian, Eton College.

93 Information from Trinity College Library, Cambridge.

94 *Paul Pry*, 1850s.

95 Martin, Robert B., *Tennyson*, 395.

96 Rendle, T. Macdonald, *Swings and Roundabouts*, 266.

97 Chesney, Kellow, *The Victorian Underworld*, 309-10.

98 Lambton, Arthur, *My Story*, 141.

99 Ailesbury Archives, Wiltshire. [AW infra.]

100 *Truth*, 7 Novemer 1878.

101 Ibid., 14 November 1878.

102 Ibid.

103 AW.

104 AW.

105 *Savernake Forest*, 308.

106 AW.

107 *Survey of London*, XL.

108 Rooke, P., ed., compiler, Mott, R., *Theobalds through the Centuries.*

109 *Portrait of Lady Meux*, Honolulu Academy of Arts, see Exhibition catalogue of *James McNeill Whistler*, R. Dorment and M.F. MacDonald, Tate Gallery, 1994, no. 124. According to J. G. Links, to whom I am grateful for the information, the cloak could only have been white arctic fox at that time though Whistler appears to have made no attempt other than to paint symbolic white fur. Forty years later Edith Wharton could write of a 'chinchilla cloak with ermine lining'. *Glimpses of the Moon*, 1922, 206.

110 *Theobalds.*

111 *Whistler*, Tate.
112 The Frick Collection, New York.
113 Glasgow University Library, M.341, 339.
114 MacDonald, Margaret F., *James McNeill Whistler, A Catalogue Raisonné*, 321.
115 *Whistler*, Tate, no. 126.
116 Ibid., no. 125.
117 Glasgow University Library, M.338.
118 *Whistler*, Tate, no. 126.
119 AW.
120 AW.
121 AW and see Part I of this book.
122 *Survey of London* XL.
123 AW.
124 AW.
125 AW.
126 Cardigan and Lancaster, *My Recollections*, 139.
127 Blumenfeld, R. D., *R.D.B.'s Diary*, 188.
128 *The Complete Peerage*.
129 AW.
130 AW.
131 *The World*, October 1886.
132 Cochran, C.B., *A Showman Looks On*, 128.
133 *Savernake Forest*, 317.
134 Rooke, P., ed., Mott, R. The hieroglyphics were acknowledged by Sir Wallis Budge, Keeper of Egyptology at the British Museum, from a papyrus.
135 Lambton, 161, 144.
136 Ibid., 145.
137 Ibid., 142.
138 Ibid., 149, 162.
139 The following account is taken from Bradburn, R., *Margaret McMillan*.
140 Lambton, 151.
141 Colville, Sir John, *Those Lambtons!*, 92.
142 Mortimer, Roger, *History of the Derby Stakes*, 349-50.

Select Bibliography

All books are published in London unless otherwise stated

Anson, P. F., *Fashions in Church Furnishings*, 1965.

Askwith, Betty, *A Victorian Young Lady,* 1978.

Barker, Kathleen, 'The Theatre Royal, Bristol', *The Society for Theatre Research*, 1974.

Barton, M., *Garrick*, 1948.

Best, Geoffrey, *Mid-Victorian Britain, 1851-1875*, 1971.

Bigland, Eileen, *Ouida, The Passionate Victorian*, 1950.

Bishop, P. T., B. D. B., and Lucas, B. G. B., edd., *The Seven Ages of the Brompton*, 1991.

Blumenfeld, R.D., *R.D.B.'s Diary*, 1930.

Bradburn, Elizabeth, *Margaret McMillan*, 1989.

Burnand, Sir Frederick, *Records and Reminiscences*, i, ii, 1904.

Burne-Jones, G., *Memorials of Edward Burne-Jones*, i, 1904.

Cardigan, Earl of, *The Wardens of Savernake Forest*, 1949.

Cardigan and Lancaster, Countess of, *My Recollections*, 1909.

Chancellor, E. Beresford, *Pleasure Haunts of London*, 1925.

Chesney, Kellow, *The Victorian Underworld*, 1970.

Cochran, C. B. *A Showman Looks On*, 1945.

Coleman, John, *Charles Reade*, 1903.

Colville, Sir John, *Those Lambtons!*, 1988.

Cook, E. T. and Wedderburn, A., edd., *The Works of John Ruskin*, XXXVI, 1909.

Davis, Tracy C., *Actresses as Working Women*, 1991.

Desmond, Shaw, *London Nights of Long Ago*, 1929.

Dorment, Richard, and MacDonald, Margaret F., *James McNeill Whistler*, Exhibition Catalogue, Tate Gallery, 1994.

Drummond, Maldwin, *Salt Lake Palaces*, 1979.
Duncan, Barry, *The St James's Theatre, 1837-1957*, 1964.
Edwards, Jack, *Cheshunt in Herfordshire*, Cheshunt Urban District Council, 1974.
Ellis, S. M., *A Mid-Victorian Pepys*, 1923.
Engen, Rodney, *John Tenniel's Alice's White Knight*, 1991.
Frith, W., *My Autobiography and Reminiscences*, i, 1887.
Green, R. Lancelyn, ed., *Diaries of Lewis Carroll*, i, 1953.
Hay, C., *The Club and the Drawing Rooms*, 1870.
Hibbert, H. G., *Fifty Years of a London Life*, 1916.
Hibbert, H. G., *A Playgoer's Memoirs*, 1920.
Hunt, Violet, Unpublished diaries, Cornell University, New York.
Irving, Laurence, *Henry Irving, The Actor and His World*, 1951.
Lambton, Arthur, *My Story*, 1925.
Lankford, Nelson D., *The Last American Gentleman*, 1996.
MacCarthy, Fiona, *William Morris*, 1994.
MacDonald, Margaret F., *James McNeill Whistler, Drawings, Pastels and Watercolours, A Catalogue Raisonné*, 1995.
Mander, Raymond, and Mitchison, J., *The Lost Theatres of London*, 1968.
Martin, Robert B., *Tennyson*, O.U.P., 1980.
Mortimer, Roger, *History of the Derby Stakes*, 1962.
Naylor, L. E., *The Irrepressible Victorian*, 1965.
Nicoll, Allardyce, *History of the English Drama*, v, vi, C.U.P., 1952-9.
Pemberton, E., *Life of T. W. Robertson*, 1893.
Phillips, P., 'The Meux Succession', unpublished typescript.
Planché, J. R., *Recollections and Reflections*, ii, 1872.
Pulver, Rosalind, 'Who Was J. D. Rochfort?', *Antique Dealer and Collector's Guide*, January 1993.
Quennell, Peter, *London's Underground World*, 1950.
Rendle, T. McDonald, *Swings and Roundabouts*, 1919.
Rooke, Peter, ed., and compiled by Mott, R., *Theobalds through the Centuries*, 1980.
Sala, G. A., *Twice Round the Clock*. 1859.
Scott, Clement, and Howard C., edd., *Life and Reminiscences of E. L. Blanchard*, i, ii, 1891.

Scott, Clement, *Thirty Years at the Play and Dramatic Table Talk*, 1892.

Scott, Clement, *Old Days in Bohemian London*, 1919.

Sherson, Erroll, *London's Lost Theatres of the Nineteenth Century*, 1925.

Southern, Richard, *The Victorian Theatre*, 1970.

Stirling, A. M. W., *A Painter of Dreams*, 1916.

Stuart, C. D., and Park, A. J., *The Variety Stage*, 1895.

Surtees, V., ed. *The Diaries of George Price Boyce*, Real World, Norwich, 1980.

Surtees, V., *The Diary of Ford Madox Brown*, Yale U. P., 1981.

Survey of London, XXXIX, XL, XLI.

Terry, Ellen, *The Story of My Life*, 2nd ed., nd.

Thompson, F. M. L., *English Landed Society in the Nineteenth Century*, 1963.

Vizetelly, H., *Glances Back through Seventy Years*, i, 1893.

Wallack, Lester, *Memories of Fifty Years*, New York, 1889.

Yates, Edmund, *Recollections and Experiences*, i, 1884.

Index

INDEX

Meux, Sir Henry Bruce (Harry), 3rd
  Baronet, seduced by Val, 105; his
  wealth, 105, 121; impending
  baronetcy, 106; family background,
  106; upbringing, 114; marriage
  which stuns his family, 118–19;
  character, 119, 120, 133; his
  honeymoon, 121; buys London
  house, 122; excavates Avebury
  while living at Dauntsey, 123; and
  deer stalking, 127; his father dies,
  133; settles at Theobalds, 143;
  turns to drink, 147, 150; death and
  burial, 133
Meux, (Lady) Louisa, wife of 2nd
  Baronet, 110, 111, 112; her
  behaviour, 112, 113, 130–1,
  136–7; lives in Paris, 113; reviles
  Harry's associates, 116, 119, and
  his wife, 121; in Switzerland, 131;
  her parents' fears of remarriage,
  137; at Mentone, 136, 137; Lord
  Henry takes charge of her, 137;
  death, 137
Meux, Valerie Suzie (Lady),
  appearance, 105, 116, 127, 146;
  background, 105–6; Whistler's
  paintings of, 124–9; characteristics,
  105, 116, 118, 148; unacceptable
  to Society, 105, 124, 143, 149;
  meets Henry, 115, 116; on his
  yacht, 116; Corporal Reece, 117;
  marries Harry, 118; acquires
  jewellery, 121; collects antiquities,
  121, and displays them, 146; rides
  to hounds at Dauntsey, 123;
  acquires title and wealth, 132, 133;
  incident of diamond buckle,
  134–5; entertains at Theobalds,
  146–7, 150–1; engages Margaret
  McMillan, 148; influences
  elevation of Temple Bar, 152;
  inherits a fortune, 153; presents
  Dauntsey church with window,
  153–4; bowled over by Capt
  Lambton, 154; enthusiasm for
  racing, 156; altercation over lease

of Volodyovski, 156, who wins the
  Derby, 157; is hit financially, 158;
  death at Coburg Hotel, 158; her
  approximate age, 158; her will,
  158–9
Milbank, (Sir) Frederick Acclom (Bt),
  lover of Miss H., father of Midge,
  friend of Rochfort, 54; family and
  character, 54; as collector, 56;
  financial settlements made for
  Midge, 56, 97; as lessee of St
  James's Theatre, 57; takes
  responsibilty of removing play, 57,
  59; unavailable for Aurora Floyd,
  62; his seizure at Sidmouth Lodge,
  83; appraises portraits of Midge,
  85; removal to The Boltons, 89;
  mentioned in Rochfort's will, 94;
  in Vanity Fair, 97; confronted by
  Midge for further settlement, 97
Millais, John Everett, 28, 49, 93
Moore, Nelly, 53
Morris, William, 45, 49; and Morris
  Firm, 89
Morris, Mrs William, 37, 90
Mountbatten, Countess, 158
Munro, Alexander, 28

Olympic Theatre, 26–7, 29; Miss H.'s
  Benefit at, 44–5
Ouida, 75–6

Planché, J. R., 70
Potter, Beatrix, 90
Pottow, John, 19
Pottow, Mrs John (Emma Maynard),
  birth and upbringing, 15, 16;
  marriage and family, 19; her age
  and death, 19; witness to Crabb's
  impropriety, 30–1; her mother's
  death, 50; testifies against Crabb,
  81; ministers to Milbank, 83
Princess's Theatre, 62, 73
Prinsep, Mr and Mrs Thoby, 39
Prinsep, Valentine Cameron, 37,
  49
Punch, 29, 57, 71

[174]